STAFF RECRUITMENT AND RETENTION

STRATEGIES FOR EFFECTIVE ACTION

ALASTAIR EVANS

Chandos Publishing

Oxford · England

Chandos Publishing (Oxford) Limited
Chandos House
5 & 6 Steadys Lane
Stanton Harcourt
Oxford OX8 1RL
England
Tel: +44 (0) 1865 882727 Fax: +44 (0) 1865 884448
Email: sales@chandospublishing.com
www.chandospublishing.com

••

First published in Great Britain in 2001

ISBN 1 902375 72 6

© A. Evans, 2001

Typeset by Turn-Around Typesetting
Printed by Biddles, Guildford, UK

Contents

....

PART 1   RECRUITMENT AND SELECTION

Introduction

This book is concerned with two of the most critical issues facing many organisations today: how do we recruit staff who will perform effectively in their roles and, secondly, having recruited them, how do we keep them? According to some recent research, 'the ability to attract and retain talent is rapidly becoming one of the key issues for human resource managers and their organisations across the globe' and the conclusion was that 'the ability to attract and retain staff is rapidly becoming one of the core competencies of high performance organisations' (Hiltrop, 1999: 422, 428). As evidence, the author quotes the findings of an international survey by the American Management Association conducted in 1998 which asked nearly 1,800 executives and managers from 36 countries about 65 possible business issues of current and future importance. The results showed that as a category, recruitment and retention ranked third in terms of increasing importance over the coming decade, up from fifth in 1997 (ibid.: 423).

A welter of recent surveys in Britain have similarly highlighted the current importance to organisations of recruitment and retention issues. A survey from Cranfield (2000) identified that 61% of organisations expected difficulties in recruiting senior management and professional staff, 57% expected difficulties in recruiting at board level and 52% expected difficulties recruiting at middle management level. A number of surveys have also highlighted current concerns with retention. In one survey, 53% of managers said that turnover was too high in their organisations, 50% thought that the problem had worsened over the previous two years and almost all respondents (98%) agreed that high recruitment and training costs were a consequence of high turnover (IRS, 1999b). Another survey found that almost 70% of employers said that they were experiencing retention problems and that the most widely adopted strategy for tackling them was through improvements in recruitment and selection, a strategy favoured by two-thirds of the respondents (IRS, 1999a). Further evidence comes from PricewaterhouseCoopers (2000) who identified that staff retention was the most important issue for 80% of organisations replying to their *HR Benchmarking* survey and 81% of respondents saw the solution in terms of improved employee development opportunities. Research by IRS (1999b: 5) similarly identified retention as a key issue and concluded that 'employers are increasingly accepting that labour turnover and retention need as much attention as recruitment and selection'. The report went on to quote the results of American research which showed a strong correlation between customer retention levels and low employee turnover. Companies with labour turnover at no more than 10% per annum retained 10% more customers than companies where turnover exceeded 15% (ibid.: 6).

Recruitment, retention and the new psychological contract

The reasons why recruitment and retention have emerged as more critical and important strategic issues for organisations have been explained in terms of significant changes which have taken place in what has been referred to as the 'psychological contract' between employers and employees during the 1990s (IRS, 1999a; Hiltrop, 1999). The psychological contract may be seen in terms of unwritten understandings about what an employee can expect from an employer in return for their commitment and these implied understandings have undergone extensive change in recent years as a result of such initiatives as downsizing, delayering, flatter structures, outsourcing and the development of lean organisations (IPD, 1996; Syrett and Lammiman, 1997; IPD, 1998). Prior to these changes, the 'old' psychological contract implied job security ('a job for life'), and regular annual pay increases based on service and career progression in return for employee loyalty and service (IRS, 1999a). Thus, it provided a strategy for employee retention. The 'new' psychological contract in the wake of the changes referred to implies less job security, fewer opportunities for upward progression in flatter organisations and pay increases in return for performance. Less job security and fewer promotion opportunities clearly affect employees' assessments about staying with their current employer and the new psychological contract appears to offer a less effective strategy for employee retention. However, while employers may not be offering 'job' security in the new paradigm, many are offering 'employment' security which requires employees to be flexible and to maintain their 'employability' through a willingness to learn new skills and take on new roles often at the same level, without necessarily expecting upward progression (Walton, 1999; Sparrow and Marchington, 1998). If this is the case, then it might be expected that new strategies are needed for recruitment and retention that revolve around the need for flexibility, training and development and more innovative approaches to career development.

The costs of ineffective recruitment and retention strategies

Recruitment and the replacement of leavers involve considerable costs and improvements in relation to both offer significant opportunities for organisations to reduce these costs. A recent survey by the Chartered Institute of Personnel and Development (CIPD) indicates that the costs of labour turnover and the associated costs arising out of recruiting replacements is currently of the order of £17.5 billion per annum nationally, based on five million job changes in the external labour market at a replacement cost of £3,500 per leaver (derived from CIPD, 2000). This figure of course excludes the costs and resources involved in internal job changes. Other estimates (e.g. Fair, 1992; IDS, 1995; Cooper, 2000b) have estimated the costs at a considerably higher figure than this, putting the cost per leaver at the equivalent of between six months' and and two years' salary, with higher costs being incurred for more senior posts. Taking an estimate from the middle of this range, with the cost per leaver at the equivalent of one year's salary, this would put the annual cost of replacement across the economy as a whole at nearer £100 billion. In terms of the cost to an organisation with, say, 1,000 employees, with the national average rate of labour turnover of 18% and a national average pay rate of £20,000 per annum, the annual cost to this organisation would be a staggering £3.6 million, with potential savings of £20,000 for each 1% reduction achieved in labour turnover.

Effective recruitment and retention strategies and the 'bottom line'

Beyond the important issue of costs, there has also been a growing body of evidence arising out of research undertaken during the past three years or so which has identified direct links between aspects of human resource management practice and overall improvements in business performance, and practices in relation to both recruitment and retention have featured prominently in their findings.

As regards recruitment, an American survey by Watson Wyatt (in Overell, 1999) looked at a range of HR practices in relation to increases in the share market value of the organisation and identified 'excellence in recruiting' as the single most important contributor. By attracting the best people, 'recruiting excellence' was responsible for up to a possible 10% gain in the share market value of the organisation. This mirrored a similar finding by Pfeffer (1998) who identified the importance of concentrating resources on recruiting the right people in the first place as one of seven key areas of HR practice which enhanced the financial performance of organisations.

Similar links have been found between retention and many of the strategies for enhancing it to be considered in the second part of this book. Watson Wyatt (in Overell, 1999), for example, identified that performance management, involving performance appraisal to establish clear objectives and accountabilities linked to reward and employee development, could potentially increase an organisation's share market value by 9%. Flexible working arrangements, teamworking and attention to the design of jobs so as to motivate staff could potentially increase share market value by nearly 8%. Similarly, Pfeffer (1998), in addition to identifying 'excellence in recruitment' as one of seven key contributors to enhanced financial performance, also identified the following further HR practices as additional contributors: self-managed teams and decentralised decision-making; pay increases commensurate with organisational performance; high investment in training; security of employment; reduced status differentials; and openness of information and communication. Many of these will feature in the discussion of retention strategies in the second part of this book.

While research into the links between HR practices and 'bottom line' improvements is continuing (see, for example, Baron and Collard, 1999; Guest and Baron, 2000; Purcell et al., 2000), the evidence so far indicates that the adoption of more effective practices in relation to recruitment, together with practices associated with enhanced retention, appear to be directly linked to improvements in the financial performance of the organisation as a whole.

The book is organised in two parts. Part 1 is concerned with recruitment and selection. Chapter 1 discusses the importance of establishing clear criteria prior to commencing any recruitment and selection activity. Chapter 2 considers issues in relation to sources of recruitment and Chapter 3 discusses the main techniques for selection, focusing on the selection interview, psychometric testing and assessment centres. Part 2 of the book is concerned with strategies for retention. Its opening chapter, Chapter 4, provides an overview of the causes of labour turnover and the strategies used by organisations for enhancing retention. Subsequent chapters consider these in more detail. Chapter 5 looks at the role of effective induction in helping to ensure that new starters will stay with the organisation. Chapter 6 considers approaches to the design of jobs and the issue of motivation which many recent studies of retention have, as we shall see, identified as key to any retention strategy. Chapter 7 considers the role of performance management, encompassing target setting, reward and employee development, all of which emerge as important elements in a retention strategy. The final chapter considers the recently emerging debate about the 'work–life balance', which includes such issues as 'flexible' and 'family-friendly' policies, and examines the role these can potentially play in retaining staff.

About the author

Alastair Evans is course director of the CIPD programme and senior lecturer in human resource management at Thames Valley University, London. He holds the degree of MA in Industrial Relations from the University of Warwick and is a fellow of the CIPD. Prior to his current post, he was a personnel director in the computer software industry and before that an HR consultant in the same industry. He also worked for the former Institute of Personnel Management for a number of years as a policy adviser in the field of employee resourcing. Over the past 20 years he has published more than a dozen books on a variety of aspects of human resource management, including human resource planning, computerised personnel systems, data protection, flexible work patterns and absence management. He has also been for some years a consulting editor of the Croner.CCH publication *British Personnel Management*.

The author may be contacted via the publishers.

PART 1

Recruitment and Selection

CHAPTER 1

Preparing to recruit

Recruitment and selection can be seen in terms of five distinct phases:

- considering alternative options before deciding to recruit at all;

- defining the criteria against which candidates are to be selected;

- attracting suitably qualified candidates;

- screening and shortlisting to eliminate unsuitable candidates;

- selecting and appointing candidates who provide the best match with the criteria defined using one or more of a range of selection tools available.

After considering whether the vacancy needs to be filled at all or whether it provides opportunities for alternative ways of fulfilling the role, the next stage is to establish criteria against which the vacancy will be filled if it has been determined that a new incumbent will be sought. On the basis of recent research into improving the effectiveness of the the recruitment and selection process as a more accurate predictor of the future performance of candidates, the importance of establishing clear and measurable selection criteria cannot be overemphasised. Having established the criteria, in terms of the responsibilities and in terms of the attributes or competencies required of an effective performer, the remainder of the recruitment and selection process becomes 'criteria-driven'. The criteria established will be relevant to the content of the job advertisement, will provide the sole yardstick against which candidates are sifted and shortlisted, and will form the basis upon which interview questions will be determined, psychometric tests selected and assessment centre exercises devised. This chapter is concerned with what needs to be done when preparing to recruit, in particular the roles of job analysis, job descriptions, person specifications and competency profiles in generating selection criteria. Chapter 2 will be concerned with methods and sources of recruitment and Chapter 3 with the three most important techniques of selection: interviews, psychometric tests and assessment centres.

Considering alternative options

Whenever a vacancy arises as a result of a resignation, it is important to consider whether the organisation has any alternative and more cost-effective options which may obviate the need to replace the role vacated in exactly its current form. These options include the following (Torrington and Hall, 1998: 205):

- *Reorganise the work*. One option is to reorganise and redistribute the current workload among the existing staff. Opportunities may exist to delegate tasks previously performed by the departing incumbant among various members of staff. Another, especially where a range of related tasks is performed by members of a team, is to question current demarcations between team members and move to a more flexible, multi-skilled approach in which staff learn to perform each other's roles. Increased multi-skilling, especially where the team as a whole is working below capacity, can facilitate non-replacement when a team member leaves.

- *Subcontract the work*. When a job incumbant leaves, a question may be asked as to whether it is necessary to replace them on the basis of a permanent employment contract. Also known as 'distancing' or 'outsourcing', this is an option which many organisations have found increasingly attractive and, in effect, employment contracts are replaced by commercial contracts with suppliers of specialist staff. Most organisations have now replaced traditional employment contracts in such areas as catering, cleaning, security, building maintenance and so on with commercial contracts with specialist providers, with the advantages of saving on employment overhead costs and avoiding the legal obligations implied in a contract of employment.

- *Employ temporary staff*. This may form part of the strategy of subcontracting, as noted above, where former permanent positions become filled by temporary agency staff. Roles may also be filled by temporary staff where forthcoming organisational changes, such as anticipated redundancies, will enable vacancies to be filled by internal rather than external applicants.

- *Make the job part-time.* Recent years have seen a growth in part-time working and a trend towards employing part-timers in positions which would formerly have been seen as open only to full-timers. Replacing a full-time vacancy by a part-timer may be particularly appropriate where the time of the previous full-time incumbant was underutilised.

- *Mechanise the work.* Though mechanisation is rarely a decision that is taken as an immediate response to a vacancy arising, clearly technological innovations over a period of time do offer opportunities to mechanise or automate work previously carried out manually and reduce or obviate the need for direct replacements.

- *Use overtime.* It is possible to cover workloads created by unfilled vacancies through the use of additional overtime working among existing staff and this may be a short-term response to avoiding permanent vacancy filling where there is some uncertainty about future workloads, for example at a time of anticipated economic downturns. Given, however, the costs of overtime working at premium rates, this is unlikely to provide a longer-term solution to avoiding vacancy filling.

Though many of the above initiatives could be considered at the time a vacancy arises, most are better implemented on a carefully planned basis and are often best given careful consideration as part of an organisation's human resource planning processes.

Defining selection criteria

According to a recent survey of recruitment practices among 2,000 employers in central London (Focus, 2000), the main issue to emerge in the view of the researchers was the failure of employers to decide exactly what skills they wanted before the recruitment process began. In consequence, the survey concluded, 'employers in London are lowering their chances of recruiting the right candidates in an already tight market because they are unclear what they are looking for'. The survey confirms what has long been suspected: defining clear criteria is often the most neglected part of the recruitment and selection process. The decision to recruit a new employee, whether to replace one who has resigned or to fill a newly created position, is often taken with ill-considered haste and without due consideration of the requirements of the position or the attributes of candidates likely to be best fitted to perform the role effectively. This is likely to result in disappointment on the part of both the organisation and the new recruit and exacerbate problems of retention and motivation. The task of defining selection criteria can range from the highly sophisticated to the relatively simple. The former is likely to be more appropriate in larger organisations with access to the expertise of specialist human resource practitioners and the latter likely to be more relevant in smaller organisations without access to such resources. Set out below are what may be seen as ideal approaches, followed by a brief discussion of what may be achieved using less sophisticated methods.

Job analysis

Job analysis is concerned with establishing the tasks and responsibilities that make up a role and also with defining the attributes and qualities of the person performing the role. The former results in a job description and the latter a person specification or, increasingly, a competency profile. The overall purpose of the exercise is to establish criteria against which to assess all candidates in relation to their expertise to perform the tasks required and their underlying attributes in relation to those perceived as central to performing the role effectively. Thus, job analysis and its outputs, job descriptions, person specifications or competency profiles, become the drivers behind what has come to be referred to as structured and criteria or competency-based recruitment and selection. For reasons which will be explained below, research has shown that this approach is more likely to result in the selection of candidates who will prove effective in the role than more traditional and less systematic methods (Janz et al., 1986; Latham, 1989).

Job analysis may be carried out by specialist consultants or human resource practitioners, but there are many benefits to be gained by maximising the involvement of line managers, supervisors and employees themselves in the process and delegating much of the task of job analysis to them. This can be achieved by documenting a framework for guidance and providing some training in its use. It will be evident that a full programme of job analysis will call for investment in time, resources and training in order for it to be conducted effectively. Given, however, the potential gains to be had from more effective recruitment and selection decisions, these need to be weighed against the costs to be incurred.

Information to be gathered in job analysis

A range of methods is available for conducting job analysis and these will be summarised in the next section. Whichever method is used it is important to bear in mind the twin objectives of job analysis noted above – to gather information about both the content of the job and the characteristics of effective performance. A number of frameworks have been offered as guides to the information-gathering process, including the following.

The Position Analysis Questionnaire (Pearn and Kandola, 1993) proposes that the following categories of information should be sought:

- the sources of information used to perform the job;

- the kind of mental processes used to perform the job;

- the output expected and methods used;

- the types and levels of relationships with others (internally and externally);

- the physical and social context in which the job is performed;

- other relevant job characteristics (e.g. non-standard patterns of working hours, travel or mobility requirements, etc.).

Another checklist has been offered by Corbridge and Pilbeam (1998, 79) which consists of the following:

- data which identifies the job and locates it in the organisation structure;

- job objectives and performance measures;

- accountabilities, responsibilities and organisational relationships;

- job duties and content;

- terms of employment and work conditions;

- skills, knowledge, qualities and competencies required;

- other distinctive job characteristics.

A final checklist has been offered by Torrington and Hall (1991: 248–9) which contains the following elements:

1. Job identification data, e.g. job title, department, division, location.

2. Relationships with others, e.g. to whom the post reports, for whom the job holder is responsible, internal and external contacts and their level of seniority.

3. Job content, including the main purpose of the job, its tasks or duties, the levels of responsibility and importance of tasks and how often they are performed.

4. Working conditions, including the physical environment, whether the work is performed largely alone or is integrated into a team and any unusual hours or patterns of work.

5. Performance standards or objectives and what behaviours are used in order to achieve them.

6. Other relevant information.

7. Human requirements in terms of the skills, knowledge, experience, etc. (as considered in more detail under 'person specifications' below).

While there are some differences and some overlaps between these checklists, organisations may wish to tailor a specific set of criteria appropriate to their needs. Further frameworks for guiding the information for collection in job analysis are given in the section on 'person specifications' below. These include the 'Seven-Point Plan', the 'Five-Fold Grading', the 'Six-Factor Formula' and the 'PERSON' specification. While these have been developed specifically to guide the content of a person specification, they also provide relevant checklists about information to be gathered in job analysis and thus it is possible to select factors from all these checklists to meet the needs of a specific organisation, while at the same time ensuring that a balance is maintained between information about the duties and the person required.

Methods of job analysis

A range of data gathering methods is available, some of the leading ones being as follows. The most widely used is interviewing, with questions being designed around the categories of data selected for gathering (as noted above) and being put to job holders and their bosses, and possibly also their peers and subordinates. Two specific techniques are often used in job analysis interviews, known as the 'critical incident' and 'repertory grid' techniques (Roberts, 1997).

Rather than start with a pre-defined checklist, as described above, the critical incident technique, originally developed by Flanagan (1954), starts by asking the job holder to identify the key objectives or 'key result areas' of the job and then involves asking the job holder to recount specific examples of how they handled these in practice. Where objectives were met or not met, the interviewer can then explore the interviewee's explanations and build up a picture of the kind of behaviours that lead to more successful or less successful outcomes. As we shall see later, this information can also be used as the basis for establishing a competency framework. Critical incident techniques may also be used to interview the bosses of job holders in order to further extend the picture of what key decisions are taken and what more effective or less effective behaviours are deployed in its performance. The method also has the advantage that it focuses on those aspects of performance that make a critical difference to effective performance, rather than focusing on the more routine and less critical aspects of the role.

The repertory grid approach to job analysis interviewing, based on a concept first developed by Kelly (1955), similarly starts with the key objectives of the job and seeks to identify the underlying skills or abilities underpinning more effective or less effective performance. While various methods of repertory grid analysis are available, a relatively straightforward use of it is to interview managers in order to obtain their assessments of employee performance in relation to various job objectives. Taking each of the job objectives in turn, the manager is asked to consider specific staff whom they have managed, either currently or in the past, and to provide examples from their experience of how a more effective employee performed in relation to objectives and how a less effective employee performed (Roberts, 1997). The approach can also be combined with the critical incidents technique to provide a focus on the critical decisions taken in the job. At the end of the process, this technique will help to build up a profile of what more effective or less effective performers actually do in performing their roles. As we shall see, all of this evidence will form an essential part of the assessment process when making selection decisions, with the central objective being to identify those behaviours, as related by candidates, that most closely match those we have identified as effective as a result of job analysis.

In addition to interviewing, a number of further methods of job analysis are also available (Roberts, 1997). These include:

- standardised questionnaires and checklists for completion by job holders or job holders in conjunction with their managers;

- work diaries or logs in which job holders record their daily tasks and decisions taken and the time spent on each;

- observation of job holders;

- the use of focus groups which involves bringing together each work group and their manager to analyse the tasks performed by group members and to brainstorm the attributes of effective performance, possibly also deploying the critical incident and repertory grid techniques noted above.

Once all the raw data has been gathered from the process of job analysis, it needs to be summarised in a standard format. The format will clearly reflect the categories of information gathered in the job analysis, with the tasks and duties being summarised in a job description and the qualities and attributes of job holders being summarised in either a person specification or a competency profile (or possibly both). It is to the drafting of these documents that we now turn.

Job descriptions

Job analysis provides the source of the data for the job description, but in order to help ensure some consistency a number of conventions have been suggested when compiling them. The first of these relates to their content in terms of subsections on which there is general agreement (see, for example, Ungerson, 1983, or Fowler, 2000) that these should be as follows:

- *Job title.* This should be clear and jargon-free so as to be generally understood by potential job applicants and adequately reflect the responsibilities, taking care not to exaggerate or inflate the role (which may only result in misleading job applicants and eventually job holders).

- *Location.* Both geographic location and department.

- *Reporting relationships.* The job description should state the title of the job to which a job holder reports. This will usually be a single post, but where there is, for example, a 'dotted line' relationship to another job holder, the respective reporting relationships and responsibilities need to be clearly stated. It should also contain a list of posts for which the job holder is directly responsible (if any). The emphasis here is on *direct* responsibility; where the post is, for example, a head of a department, this will not include all the employees in the department but only those directly supervised.

- *Overall purpose.* Usually commencing with an active verb (e.g. 'to advise', 'to monitor', 'to control', etc.), this section aims to encapsulate in a single sentence if possible why the job exists and should also adequately reflect the key tasks and responsibilities considered in the next section.

- *Key tasks and responsibilities.* These lie at the heart of the job description and are also referred to as 'principal accountabilities' or 'key result areas' and are likely to reflect those critical areas of decision-making revealed through the use of the 'critical incidents' technique discussed above. The content of the key tasks and responsibilities section of the job description should avoid becoming an exhaustive listing of everything that is or could be done down to the minutest detail. It is often suggested that no more than ten key areas need appear and less for more junior posts, with the general recommendation being that job descriptions which run to many pages are unnecessary and inappropriate. Bear in mind that one important use of the job description in criteria-based selection will be to form questions designed to assess a candidate's suitability to perform the critical aspects of the role. By restricting the job description to the most important elements in the role, this will highlight for interviewers the areas to be explored within a context of limited time. As with job purpose, the convention when setting out the key tasks and responsibilities is to commence with an action verb, stating succinctly both what is done and why it is done, but avoiding the detail of how it is done, e.g. 'to monitor quality of output so as to ensure conformance to specified quality targets'. Thus, key tasks and responsibilities should be expressed in a form in which measures may be applied (e.g. volumes, costs, speed, accuracy, quality standards, timescales, etc.). Note, however, that it is not necessary in job descriptions to state what a specific measure is unless there are resources available to update the job description each time these change. Job descriptions define the nature of the responsibility and the generic measure that will be applied. Other organisational control processes, such as target- or objective-setting, often associated with performance appraisal set in the context of departmental and corporate objectives, provide a more appropriate framework for setting and assessing specific measures and these are discussed further in Chapter 7 below.

The case has been put for brevity in job descriptions and it is potentially open to the criticism that employees may be reluctant to undertake tasks not actually specified. In practice, it is probably more likely that this might occur where jobs are defined in intricate detail and very carefully delineated. However, aware of this potential problem, many organisations do add a 'catch all' at the end of the list of tasks and responsibilities in the job description, adding the requirement that the job holder will also perform such other duties as may reasonably be required from time to time.

Person specifications

While the job description summarises the data about the tasks generated by job analysis, the person specification draws together and summarises the qualities and attributes required of the effective performer. In many respects, therefore, it is the more critical of the two documents setting out the selection criteria.

Essential and desirable requirements in the person specification

It is usual that the person specification for each post, like the job description, will conform to a standard format which reflects the generic categories of attributes identified in the job analysis. Some person specifications set out attributes that are 'essential' and those that are 'desirable' and if this type of format is required, then this information must be sought as part of the data-gathering in job analysis (e.g. by asking managers or employees to specify what are seen as essential or desirable attributes in job holders). Essential characteristics (e.g. skills, abilities, knowledge, experience, qualifications, etc.) should include only those requirements without which a potential job holder would be unable to perform one aspect or another of the key tasks or responsibilities. Desirable characteristics will include areas of knowledge or experience etc. which it is felt will enhance the potential job holder's standard or quality of performance in one or more of the tasks or responsibilities. The important issue when specifying either essential or desirable requirements is that they should not be overstated. Their purpose is to assist in the shortlisting process, with candidates unable to meet the essential requirements in full being rejected after the first sift, but any overstatement of essential or desirable requirements could lead to either the rejection of candidates who could have performed effectively or to the appointment of candidates who are overqualified to perform the role.

Frameworks for person specifications

The standardised content of the person specification will reflect the attributes systematically explored or emerging from the process of job analysis. Some relevant frameworks were considered above. A variety of frameworks have specifically been offered for person specifications, all of which could incorporate both essential and desirable requirements, and it is to these that we now turn. The two best-known and longest established frameworks are Rodger's 'Seven-Point Plan' (Rodger, 1952) and Munro Fraser's 'Five-Fold Grading' (Munro Fraser, 1954). The Seven-Point Plan proposes that human attributes should be documented in a person specification according to the following:

- physical make-up, e.g. physical build or strength, speech, manner, appearance, etc.;

- attainments, e.g. education, qualifications, experience, vocational training;

- general intelligence;

- special aptitudes, e.g. aptitudes with regard to written or oral communication, social or interpersonal skills, technical, mechanical, linguistic, numerical skills, etc.;

- interests, under which a profile of an applicant's hobbies or leisure pursuits is established and from which conclusions may be drawn about possible interrelationships between these and desirable job attributes or behaviours;

- disposition – in effect a profile of the likely personality of a candidate best fitted to the job role;

- circumstances, which would include such factors as domestic circumstances, family commitments, distance to travel, etc. which might impinge positively or negatively on a candidate's performance or on their propensity to stay or leave.

Munro Fraser's 'Five-Fold Grading' has some parallels with the Seven-Point Plan and proposes that the following factors should be considered in a person specification:

- impact on others – similar to Rodger's 'physical make-up' and including an individual's appearance, speech and manner;

- qualifications and experience – as in Rodger's 'attainments';

- innate abilities – as in Rodger's 'special aptitudes';

- motivation, involving a profile of the goals and ambitions likely to be displayed by successful candidates;

- emotional adjustment – broadly similar to Rodger's 'disposition', profiling likely sources of stress or other challenges in the role against which the candidate's coping abilities will be assessed.

While these frameworks have been set out because they are long-established (having been around for 50 years), well-known and probably for this reason quite widely used, they need to be treated with considerable caution in the light of the changed social and legal environment, together with the diverse and flexible labour market that has emerged since they were first conceived (Marchington and Wilkinson, 2000; Corbridge and Pilbeam, 1998). Prescribing job requirements in terms of physical attributes or domestic circumstances could lead, either consciously or unconsciously, to the establishment of criteria that may serve to discriminate against otherwise suitably qualified applicants and expose the employer to action at an employment tribunal. Profiling candidates on the basis of non-work activities will be seen by many as intrusive and also as a potential source of interviewer bias when these matters arise in discussion. There are questions too, beyond the scope of this book, about intelligence and work performance, the measurement of personality and the measurement of aptitudes, all of which raise further potential issues with these frameworks. Thus, the general conclusion is that where person specifications have already been drawn up using these frameworks, they may need close scrutiny and possibly complete revision.

There are some more recent frameworks which overcome the difficulties outlined and might instead be considered. Corbridge and Pilbeam (1998) offer what they term a 'six-factor formula'. In their view, it is important to consider two key questions when formulating the content of a person specification. First, what are the characteristics essential for effective performance of the job and, secondly, can they be measured or assessed in the recruitment and selection process? Their six-factor formula contains the following elements:

1. Skills, knowledge and competencies specifically related to job needs.

2. Personality characteristics considered essential for effective performance.

3. The length, level and type of experience necessary for effective performance.

4. Certificated qualifications.

5. Physical characteristics (if relevant).

6. Development potential: where it is expected that a postholder will have the potential to develop further and take on more responsibility in the future, some assessment of this will be required in the recruitment and selection process and will need inclusion in the person specification.

Roberts (1997) has offered the acronym 'PERSON' as a framework for person specifications containing the following characteristics:

1. **P**ersonal qualities and attributes inherent in the person's character.

2. **E**xperience, including particular types of work, level of work, type of industry, etc.

3. **R**ecord of achievement, i.e. evidence of successful achievement of projects or tasks.

4. **S**kills or qualifications needed to perform the role.

5. **O**rganisation-match, which may include the style and culture of the organisation or any specific requirements of the role, such as unusual hours or patterns of work or travelling requirements.

6. **N**eeds and expectations of the candidate, both from the job holder's and the organisation's perspectives, e.g. long-term career development or short-term fill-in.

Competencies

The notion of competencies has become increasingly influential in recent years as a tool in recruitment and selection (and, indeed, in many other areas of human resource management practice, including employee development, performance appraisal and reward management) and appears to have been adopted by between a third and a half of employers (Armstrong and Baron, 1998; IPD, 1999). The role of competencies in recruitment and selection is to supplant a competency framework for the traditional person specification, though some organisations continue to use both tools. The exact definition of competencies has been open to some debate, both in theory and practice. From a US perspective, Boyatzis (1982) sees 'competency' (plural 'competencies') in terms of the 'underlying characteristic of an individual which is causally related to effective or superior performance' and in effect is concerned with a range of characteristics, including such innate attributes as personality traits, aptitudes and attitudes, as well as skills, knowledge and behaviours in relation to task performance (Spencer and Spencer, 1993; Reid and Barrington, 1994). In the UK, 'competence' (plural 'competences') has been closely linked to the NVQ framework and has been defined by the Training Agency as 'things that a person who works in a given occupational role should be able to do' and is related to 'an action, behaviour or outcome that the person should be able to demonstrate' (in Roberts, 1997), i.e. in terms of observable behaviours with a focus on what people actually do in their work that leads to effective performance. The 'competency' approach is more focused on inputs to a job and the 'competence' approach more concerned with outputs. While the distinction between the two perspectives is quite clear, in Roberts' view 'the approaches have tended to merge in UK companies' leading to a 'hybrid approach' (1997: 70–1). While the establishment of 'competences' involves the use of 'functional analysis' which analyses tasks and their functions and matches these to relevant elements in the NVQ framework (Armstrong and Baron, 1998), competency analysis involves the use of the techniques of job analysis discussed above, in particular critical incidents and repertory grid analysis (ibid.). Both approaches incorporate the notion of effective job behaviours and since both functional analysis and the tools of job analysis generate behavioural information, they provide specific criteria against which to assess candidates through appropriate interview questions and through assessment centre exercises designed to simulate the behaviours in practice. Since the 'competency' perspective also emphasises the importance of underlying personality and aptitudes, the use of psychometric tests becomes relevant. The competency-based approach, in particular, provides an important tool in recruitment and selection because it has been based upon analysis of attributes and behaviours which have proved more effective or less effective in a given organisational context and thus identifies not only the criteria for assessment, but also yardsticks against which to assess candidate responses or performance. As we shall see later, competencies lend themselves particularly well to a structured, criteria-based approach to selection interviewing.

Defining selection criteria in the smaller organisation

It will be evident from the foregoing discussion that establishing meaningful selection criteria, with the central objective of enhancing the likelihood that the best-fitted candidate will be selected, will be costly and time-consuming. The process of job analysis leading to the generation of job descriptions and person specifications calls for considerable time and resources, even more so where it is to be extended to include a competency framework. While these approaches offer significant potential for improving the success rate of the recruitment and selection process, the resources required may be beyond those available to smaller organisations. Yet, their need to make the right decisions is as great. Rather than engaging in an extensive exercise of job analysis generating job descriptions and person specifications or competency profiles for all posts, a step-by-step approach may be adopted, with particular attention being paid to the establishment of recruitment and selection criteria when a vacancy arises, whether it is to be filled externally or internally. It is important that establishing the criteria contains the essential elements of the processes described above. At the very least, some analysis of the requirements of the job and the postholder should be established in an interview with the manager concerned and the results of this should be recorded directly into a job description and a person specification. The general principles for drafting job descriptions, as set out above, should be followed. One of the frameworks for drafting a person specification, as set out above, or possibly some combination of the attributes suggested which are felt to meet the organisation's needs should be adopted and the manager's views sought in the interview. If the manager is also able to provide some examples of effective work behaviours, particularly those seen as absolutely critical to effective performance, this would provide additional information which can be used to assess candidates at selection interviews. This process need not take long, but should at least help to clarify what qualities the organisation is seeking in a successful candidate and if combined with the use of structured behavioural interviewing, as described below, should help considerably to enhance the effectiveness of the selection process.

Specifying recruitment and selection criteria in practice

According to the IPD's *Recruitment* survey (1999), the following practices regarding the establishment of recruitment and selection criteria were identified in respondent organisations:

- 94% used formal job descriptions to identify the tasks and duties of posts to be filled.

- 88% used person specifications containing the qualities, skills, experience and qualifications required of job holders (though the use of both person specifications and job descriptions declined to two-thirds of smaller organisations).

- Just over half of organisations (51%) said that they used competency frameworks.

- Almost all organisations (97%) held discussions with line managers about the requirements of the post to be filled and almost two-thirds (65%) also extended these discussions to the current postholder or their colleagues.

In terms of the factors used and their relative importance as criteria for selection specified when the vacancy arose, the following responses were obtained in relation to managerial appointments:

- formal qualifications (mentioned by 73%);

- relevant experience (50%);

- personal qualities (34%);

- technical skills (30%);

- knowledge of relevant products and services (20%).

When assessing relevant experience, which was seen as the most important criterion, around half of respondents (48%) favoured experience in the same type of industry, while just under a third (31%) emphasised experience in the same type of job, regardless of industry.

CHAPTER 2

Methods of recruitment

While in popular parlance we may talk of recruiting new staff and blur the distinction between recruitment and selection, recruitment and selection are quite separate processes and each performs a distinct function. Recruitment refers to the process of generating a field of candidates (internally or externally) from which to make selection decisions and selection is concerned with the use of various tools, most frequently application forms or CVs and interviews, in order to sift, shortlist and appoint candidates from the field generated through the recruitment process.

Prior to commencing any recruitment activity, it is important to check that we have assembled the appropriate documentation, have appropriate systems in place for processing candidates efficiently and have observed organisational procedures designed to control the appointment of new staff. While recruitment and the subsequent selection process should not be conducted with undue haste, it is important that decisions are made promptly and without unnecessary delay because good candidates do not remain in the field for long. It is also important to bear in mind that recruitment and selection should be seen as a two-way process between the organisation and the candidate. From the organisation's perspective, it is about the process of finding a new employee for a role. But the process also needs to be viewed from the candidate's perspective – they too are making selection decisions and will be influenced by the manner in which the organisation conducts its recruitment and selection and by the information that they are given to help their decision (Herriott, 1989).

Before placing our vacancy with a recruitment agency or in the press, it will be necessary to ensure that the following have been completed, though the exact procedures may vary from organisation to organisation:

- Selection criteria have been documented. As described earlier, a job description and person specification or competency profile needs to have been prepared; in order to help the candidate make a decision, these can usefully be provided to the applicant.

- A pack of information has been prepared and made available to candidates providing realistic information about the culture or values of the organisation, career prospects, promotion, training and development opportunities, the salary, and information about the recruitment and selection process.

- A decision has been taken on whether candidates will be required to apply using an application form or CV (see below for a further discussion of this).

- Observance of procedures relating to budgets and authorisation to fill a vacancy.

- A system, probably computerised, for tracking applications and generating prompt replies.

- A decision has been taken about the closing date for applications and possibly also the dates when interviews will be held in order that the time of busy managers can been set aside in advance.

Internal and external vacancy filling

When seeking to fill vacancies which arise, organisations need to weigh the advantages and disadvantages of filling internally against filling externally. The advantages of filling internally include the following (Torrington and Hall, 1998):

- aids retention and motivation of current staff through the provision of promotion and career development opportunities;

- the candidates are better known to the organisation and the risks involved in appointing an internal candidate compared with an external one may be reduced;

- the process is likely to be speedier than external recruitment;

- recruitment costs will be considerably lower (unless an external replacement has to be found for the vacancy created by the internal appointment);

- internal candidates will already be familiar with the organisation and thus induction time and the effects of the 'learning curve' will be less, enabling an internal candidate to settle into their role more quickly.

Despite the significant benefits to be had from a policy of giving preference to internal candidates, these need to be weighed against some potential disadvantages which include the following (Torrington and Hall, 1998):

- a limited field of candidates may be available compared with the wide pool potentially available in the external labour market;

- a lack of injection of new ideas and perspectives which external candidates may bring to the organisation;

- missed opportunities to test the market and compare the quality of candidates available on the external market with those available internally.

There are broadly three policy perspectives which organisations can adopt in relation to internal and external vacancy filling. The first is to adopt the position that all vacancies will be advertised internally and internal candidates will in effect be given preferential treatment. Provided that a candidate is identified who broadly meets the criteria, an appointment will be made without going externally, with the latter being the fallback position where no internal candidate can be identified. This approach maximises the benefits of internal vacancy filling noted above, but also suffers from the key disadvantages outlined. Some organisations adopting this approach also make undertakings that all internal applicants will be interviewed and this can lead to a fruitless expenditure of time and resources, especially where it is fairly obvious from the outset that there are no suitably qualified internal candidates available. A further point to note about an excessive reliance on internal vacancy filling from an equal opportunities perspective is that it fails to open up vacancies to the wider community and where the make-up of the current workforce is predominantly white or male, this might constitute indirect discrimination under the Sex Discrimination Act 1975 or the Race Relations Act 1976.

A second approach is to advertise internally and externally in parallel. This compromises some of the advantages of internal recruitment outlined, all the more so where external candidates tend to be appointed more frequently, but has the merit that the organisation is able to assess internal candidates with those available in the market and make an optimum decision.

The third approach is that there is no formally declared policy and management decides each case on its merits, deciding to go internally or externally or do both in parallel according to the circumstances. While compromising on some of the benefits of giving priority to internal candidates, this has the advantage that the external market will be tested where felt appropriate and avoids any need to 'go through the motions' of seeing internal candidates who are clearly not fitted to the role.

Sources of applicants

Recruitment is essentially concerned with marketing a vacancy to a well-defined and targeted audience so as to generate a sufficient response from appropriately qualified applicants as cost effectively as possible (Roberts, 1997). Thus the starting point involves thorough research of the market in order to identify:

- the level of pay and benefits that will be sufficiently competitive to attract applicants;

- the typical job search behaviours of potential applicants in the market, and the advantages, disadvantages and costs of the alternative sources available for attracting applicants, given that cost constraints imposed by the organisation may limit the options that may potentially be available.

Thus, for example, if an advert is to be placed in a national newspaper, it is vital to understand the make-up of its readership and the proportion of the total readership likely to have any interest in an advertised vacancy. This will involve obtaining data based on readership research from the newspaper concerned or by consulting *British Rate and Data* where such information is summarised. If a recruitment agency is to be used, it is important to find out whether the use of agencies reflects typical job search behaviour within the targeted population for a given vacancy. While the press and recruitment agencies are the most important sources of external recruitment according to the CIPD's recruitment survey (1999), various other media are available. The sections which follow review the range of sources for recruitment and weigh the advantages and disadvantages of each.

Employment agencies

These fall into two broad types, the public sector provision through the 'JobCentres' and the commercial provision which extends from 'high street' agencies for manual and more junior white-collar staff, through recruitment agencies and consultants for technical, professional and managerial staff, to executive search consultants or 'headhunters' for more senior staff. The nature of the provision from each of these agencies will be outlined below.

JobCentres

Based in the centres of most large towns, government JobCentres are successful in targeting large numbers of jobseekers, many of whom will be unemployed. They also provide their services free of charge and in addition will provide assistance with the preparation of job descriptions and person specifications, help with screening and shortlisting and also provide interviewing facilities if required. Their database services enable searches to be conducted in relation to employers' skills requirements and the search facility extends nationally to all other JobCentres and also internationally within the European Union, and they also provide a recruitment service for executive and professional vacancies. Their main disadvantage is that their registers often contain unemployed people rather than those in work and actively seeking a job change (Corbridge and Pilbeam, 1998; Torrington and Hall, 1998).

Commercial employment agencies

The commercial sector may be subdivided into the 'high street' employment agencies generally dealing with all levels of manual worker and white-collar staff up to supervisor level and charging in the region of 10 to 15% of an annual salary for filling a position; recruitment agencies or recruitment consultancies specialising in technical, management, executive and professional staff, charging fees in the range of 18 to 25% of annual salary; and executive 'search' consultants, also known as 'headhunters', who specialise in finding candidates for senior positions, charging 30% or more of annual salary, often payable in three stages: one-third on acceptance of the search brief, one-third on producing a shortlist of acceptable candidates and the final third after appointment. Agencies' terms of business usually provide for some reimbursement of the fee paid if their candidate leaves within a specified period or proves unsatisfactory during a probationary period, e.g. full reimbursement in the first month, 50% reimbursement from the second month and on a reducing scale for each further month up to a specified maximum period. A fee is also payable where a temporary employee provided by an agency becomes a member of an organisation's permanent staff. Both the scale of fees and the terms of business may be open to negotiation and more favourable terms may be available where the agency is given exclusivity (or 'sole agency') to offer candidates over a specified period of time.

Branches of the high street agencies are readily contactable in the centres of all towns of any reasonable size and will also be found listed in the local Yellow Pages directory. For many types of vacancy, typically clerical, administrative and secretarial, they have become the established channel for vacancy filling and for many staff seeking employment in a local area have become the first port of call. In comparison with the use of the local press, which is the main alternative for filling lower level vacancies, they also offer testing, sifting and shortlisting services which reduce the administrative burden of recruitment on employers. Their disadvantage in comparison with the local press is that the target audience for a given vacancy is limited to those actually on their registers, whereas a local press advertisement will potentially reach a much wider audience, including those not actively seeking new employment. The cost of the agency will also be greater than most usual local press adverts, but it does need to be borne in mind that press adverts, unlike agency services, have to be paid for whether or not a vacancy is filled and there are likely to be additional administrative costs in processing applicants from an advert which need to be considered in any cost comparison.

Recruitment agencies or consultants specialising in technical, management and professional appointments require further research to identify who and where they are. Some of these agencies specialise by industry sector, some by occupational group and some may effectively do both. One way of identifying them is to look at which agencies are actively advertising in the national or regional press; another method is to look at any industry-based press media (e.g. *The Grocer* in retailing or *The Caterer* in the hospitality sector) to identify agencies who specialise on a sector basis; another method is to look at journals which are targeted at an occupational group (e.g. *People Management* and *Personnel Today* targeted at personnel management practitioners) and identify which agencies are actively involved in job advertising. There are also various published registers of specialist recruitment agencies which categorise their services by occupation and industry sector. The specialist agencies suffer from the same disadvantage as their high street equivalents in that the choice of candidate is limited to those registered with them, but many will undertake to place advertisements in relevant journals, sometimes at preferential rates. As with their high street equivalents, agencies have become the dominant means by which employees seek new employment in some sectors, for example in the IT sector, and in such circumstances employers are left with little alternative to using them for vacancy filling. Their benefits include shortlisting services, the ability to respond quickly, expertise in their specialist sector (including knowledge of salary market rates) and the facility to fill vacancies anonymously where this is deemed necessary, a facility which may not be available in press advertising (unless a box number is used). While their use is costly, this cost needs to be weighed in the light of advertising in the national or specialist press which (as discussed below) can also be expensive.

Executive search consultants or 'headhunters' may be located through the published recruitment directories noted above where their entries will specify whether executive search services are provided and for which sector or occupational group. Because of their high cost, their use can usually only be justified for filling senior vacancies. Their particular advantages are that they have specialist knowledge, not just of their particular sector or occupational group generally, but also of the people filling these roles, or can use networks of contacts or other search methods to identify who these people are. They also have the advantage that they are not restricted to people on their registers or people who are actively job hunting. The main reason for using executive search is that it provides highly precise targeting of potential candidates in the market and can also ensure a high degree of confidentiality and anonymity. These advantages come into their own when compared with the main alternative means of filling senior vacancies – national press advertising. If, for example, an employer is seeking to fill a vacancy for a marketing director in the pharmaceuticals sector and the incumbant sought is required to have many years experience in a major pharmaceuticals organisation and is currently occupying a senior role as, say, head of marketing, the field of candidates nationally (or even internationally) meeting these specific requirements will be relatively limited. National press advertising is an expensive way of targeting this small population and, in any event, many of them may not see the advert, particularly if they are not actively job hunting. The drawbacks of executive search are that it is expensive, that a significant fee will be payable for the search services even if no suitable candidate is found, and that suitable candidates may not be targeted where they are outside the consultant's network of contacts (Torrington and Hall, 1998).

Press advertising

Press advertising, in comparison with agencies, has the particular advantage that it reaches large audiences, but on the other side of the coin it suffers from the disadvantage of what is termed 'wastage', the extent to which the readership will actually be interested in the vacancy advertised. It is therefore important when advertising in the press that information is obtained about the make-up of its readership as a result of readership research. This information is available in the publication *British Rate and Data*. Alternatively, readership data can be obtained directly from newspaper and journal publishers. The problem of wastage can be reduced by placing advertisements in sector, trade or occupational journals, but it needs to be recognised that these may either be unsuitable or unavailable. Wastage may also be reduced where newspapers operate specialist vacancy sections on specific days. Another issue when seeking to use newspaper advertising is geographic coverage and this decision is governed by people's 'travel-to-work' habits. In general, the more junior the role and the lower the level of pay, the less people are willing or can afford to travel far to work, while the more senior and the higher the level of pay, the greater the mobility and willingness to relocate or to travel longer distances. Thus, lesser skilled manual work and more junior white-collar positions tend to be advertised in the local press. Skilled work, more senior white-collar work up to or even including management level will tend to appear in the regional press and more senior management appointments in the national press.

Other sources

While, as will be evident from the information given in the CIPD's recruitment survey below, the press and agencies are by far and away the most important sources of staff, a range of further options are also available and these are summarised below.

Universities

For many employers, the annual 'milk round' of visits to universities and undergraduate careers fairs has traditionally been an important part of their recruitment activity since graduates are a major source of staff to occupy future managerial roles. Employers also report that it is a time-consuming and expensive activity and according to the CIPD's recruitment survey (1999), fewer employers now participate in the annual milk round or graduate recruitment fairs than was formerly the case. Given that there are now nationally around 100 institutions of university status, some employers limit their search to those institutions with the highest ratings in their subjects, as published in the annual league tables which appear periodically in the press. More employers now use less costly methods than traversing the campuses, such as job advertising in undergraduate jobs bulletins or speculative applications. As an alternative strategy for obtaining graduates, employers may instead recruit A-level school leavers and sponsor them through part-time 'sandwich' courses involving periods of study and periods of work.

Schools and career centres

Local schools, the local authority career centres and government initiatives such as the New Deal (run by the local TECs) provide important sources for trainee and entry level jobs and are also relatively low-cost methods of recruitment. Employers may also establish close contact with local schools and their careers advisers who can also be a useful source of information about the candidates.

The Internet

According to Reed (2000a; 2000b), this is a rapidly growing source of recruitment, with 68% of organisations stating that they used the Internet for recruitment, an increase of 50% in a six-month period in 2000. Nearly a half of all jobseekers now look for jobs on the Internet and over 40% post their CVs on it. Reed (2000b) identifies that the Internet is now used by nearly a half of employers for graduate recruitment, by around a third for IT and technical recruitment and by around a quarter for management and professional recruitment. The most frequently cited benefits of Internet recruitment from an employer's perspective are cost, reckoned by one authority to be one-third of the cost of an equivalent press advert (Finn, 2000), and speed of response, mentioned as an advantage by 60% of employers in a survey on Internet recruiting (Reed, 2000b). In terms of disadvantages, the latter survey indicates that the use of the Internet can generate an inordinately large number of irrelevant applicants, mentioned as a problem by around 60% of employers, and a poor quality of applicants, mentioned by around 40% of employers, thus adding considerably to the administrative task of sifting and shortlisting.

Vacancy boards

These may be either internal or outside the premises and internal vacancy filling may also be associated with the use of 'finder's fees', payments of usually around £500 to employees who introduce staff who are subsequently taken on and continue to be retained after a probationary period. External vacancy boards have the added benefit that they are seen by a greater number of people than internal advertising alone, especially if the premises are on a main thoroughfare and are relatively cheap to install. The main disadvantages of the external vacancy board are that they are not well targeted in the sense that only a small number of passers-by will actually be interested, can only give basic information about a post, may attract unsuitable applicants and are not usually seen as suitable for jobs above unskilled, semi-skilled or clerical posts. The use of both internal and external vacancy boards may also be seen as indirectly discriminatory in that they do not open up vacancies to the wider community, but rather limit them to the friends and family of current employees or those living in the vicinity (Corbridge and Pilbeam, 1998). At best, such methods should be used in conjunction with other recruitment methods.

Broadcasting media

Local radio stations offer job advertising services which provide good targeting of a geographic area and, though relatively more expensive than local press advertising, may be cost-effective where a number of vacancies for a given post are to be filled at the same time. The issues with this medium relate to wastage and targeting: how many of its audience will be interested in the specific vacancy? There are also issues of getting a clear message across in a limited space of time and stimulating action: how many listeners will be equipped with paper and pen to note details down? The commercial regional television channels also offer job advertising via their teletext services, but there may be issues about public awareness of the availability of these services. Rates are comparable to larger display adverts in the regional press and the use of television may be relevant where vacancies arise on an ongoing basis or where there are a large number of vacancies to be filled.

Speculative applications and waiting lists

The results of the CIPD recruitment survey, shown below, indicate that these are widely used methods of recruitment and also have the benefits of being inexpensive and speedy in terms of vacancy filling. Waiting lists can be generated from lists of applicants from previous recruitment campaigns or from speculative CVs. In both cases, candidates should be told that their applications are being held for future consideration, but it should be noted that they also tend to have a limited 'shelf life' since applicant interest in a post will tend to decline over time as their circumstances change (Corbridge and Pilbeam, 1998). Where large numbers of applicants are held on waiting lists, retrieving lists of those with suitable qualifications and experience may require access to computerised search facilities.

Principles of effective job advertising

Wherever it has been decided to advertise in the press, there are a number of points to bear in mind when designing the advertisement in order to maximise the likelihood of achieving an acceptable response comprising suitably qualified applicants. The main aim is to reach a target audience in such a way that there are neither too many unsuitable responses, which add to the administrative cost, nor too few with suitable qualifications. It is also important to bear in mind that every advertisement makes statements about the organisation itself, whether or not those reading it have any interest in the vacancy. In many larger organisations, job advertising is seen as an integral part of public relations and its design and content may be subject to vetting by PR advisers to ensure that the desired corporate image is conveyed.

The key issues in designing job advertisements have been summarised by Ray (1980) as follows. First, it is necessary to bear in mind the functions which the advert will perform and these are as follows:

1. *To communicate with a selected audience.* Effective communication may be achieved through effective targeting of the media most likely to be seen by the target audience, as discussed above.

2. *To produce an adequate response.* This requires that the advertisement succinctly describes both the job and the requirements of the person required to fill it.

3. *To minimise wastage.* Wastage results from failing to target either a relevant medium or the required audience within that medium because of poor advertising design.

4. *To build the image of the organisation.* As noted, the appearance and content of the advertisement should do credit to the organisation and create a positive image.

As regards the aims of an advertisement, Ray suggests that it should achieve the following:

1. *Claim attention.* Given that any single advertisement usually appears buried among many others, consideration should be given to what may be done to make it stand out from others and be seen. One aspect here will relate to the size of the advertisement, with smaller adverts at lower cost likely to have less impact. Another relates to content and presentation. A well-known organisation may make the most of this by displaying their name or logo prominently on the advert. Some organisations also make use of an eye-catching headline in the advert or use an innovative design or layout, but doing these successfully usually requires the advice of specialists.

2. *Convey a story and arouse desire.* This follows on from claiming attention and it is suggested that the content of the advert should attempt to tell some story which enhances the appeal of the vacancy. This may be done by setting a context for the vacancy through the use of such phrases as 'due to expansion' or 'as a result of internal promotion' or by emphasising the challenge of the post or the excellence of the benefits or future development opportunities, etc.

3. *Stimulate action.* If the advert has performed the aims set out above, it remains important to encourage the applicant to take prompt action. This requires that the advert should clearly state what the applicant should do next and in what timescale.

As regards the specific content of the advertisement, Ray suggests that it is desirable that the following are included:

1. *The job and duties.* The job title should be unambiguous and jargon-free and be clearly understood by the potential applicant. In most job adverts, the job title forms the headline and stands out clearly from the rest of the information. It is also vital that the advert contains a brief but succinct summary of the most important duties. Without this, applicants will not be able to assess whether the vacancy appeals to them and could generate unsuitable applicants or simply put people off from applying.

2. *The name of the organisation.* People like to know who they could be working for and the organisation's name should appear. A lack of an organisation's name is likely to reduce the response rate. Unless the name of the organisation is likely to be readily known to the applicant, some brief information should also be given about the organisation itself. If confidentiality over the post and the organisation's name is such that it is omitted or perhaps a box number is used, it may be preferable to use the services of an agency rather than press advertising.

3. *They key qualities of the person required.* Just as an extract of the key duties from the job description are required, so also is an extract of the key qualities required from the person specification or competency profile, particularly those that are seen as essential, and, if space allows, reference also to those that are seen as desirable. The purpose of this is to minimise wastage by encouraging only those applicants who meet the requirements.

4. *The rewards.* A salary or salary range must be stated and phrases such as '£attractive' or 'salary negotiable' should be avoided. Adverts which fail to carry salary information are likely to result in a lower response rate. Other rewards, such as the benefit package, should also be specified, as well as such intrinsic rewards as training, development or promotion opportunities, where applicable. Salaries are sometimes omitted from adverts for confidentiality reasons, but it is suggested that the use of agencies may be preferential where confidentiality over salaries is of vital importance.

5 *Location.* The place of work must be stated and also whether there are any travel or other mobility requirements. Many applicants will have constraints on their ability to be highly mobile or to relocate and many will also want to assess the practicalities of travelling before making an application. Moreover, if it is anticipated that a future relocation will be required, this also needs stating.

6. *Action required.* Applicants must be told exactly what is required as the next step, usually by what deadline and the name of the person to whom applications must be sent. Actions may include sending a CV, telephoning or writing for an application form, telephoning for more information or in some cases telephoning in order for telephone screening to take place (see below), in which event candidates need to be advised of this.

Analysing media effectiveness and applicant monitoring

There are two reasons why the results of a recruitment campaign should be recorded. First, it provides feedback information on the cost-effectiveness of the various media used in terms of the number and quality of candidates generated as a source of information and guidance on media to be used in the future. Secondly, it helps the organisation to comply with the recommendations of the various codes of practice on equal opportunities where the gender, ethnic origin and disabilities of applicants are confidentially recorded but separated from their applicant records during shorlisting (for example, by means of tear-off slips on application forms or on separate forms). For both these purposes, the recruitment sources, costs and monitoring categories should be recorded and later analysed by:

- the number of applicants generated;

- the number of candidates progressing or failing to progress through each recruitment stage to appointment;

- the number of candidates remaining with the organisation for specified periods after appointment.

Current recruitment practices

According to the CIPD recruitment survey (1999) respondents stated that they used the following media for recruitment:

Specialist press	85%
Local press	82%
National press	72%
Employment agencies	65%
JobCentres	63%
Speculative applications	62%
Word of mouth	59%
Schools/colleges/universities	43%
Headhunters	41%
Internet	32%
Local radio	12%

The methods most commonly used for management appointments were national press advertising (used by 60% of respondents), followed by advertising in the specialist or trade press (53%) and speculative applications (48%); for professional appointments, the specialist or trade press was overwhelmingly preferred (77% of respondents); and for skilled manual workers, the most used recruitment sources were local press (68%) and the local JobCentre (59%). As regards graduate recruitment, engaged in by one-third of the employers replying, the survey found that only a minority of employers engaged in the traditional 'milk round' (23% of respondents) or graduate recruitment fairs (34%) and the preferred methods of attracting graduate applications included establishing direct contact with specific universities (64%), speculative applications (61%), using university careers' services (56%) and placing vacancies and appointments in student vacancy bulletins (50%).

As regards the typical spend by organisations on vacancy filling, *Personnel Today* reported in November 1999 that the average cost per recruit through recruitment agencies was £4,385; larger private-sector organisations employing more than 1,000 employees spent £5,021 and public-sector organisations spent £3,010 per recruit on filling vacancies through agencies.

CHAPTER 3

Techniques of selection

Selection is concerned with the processes of sifting, shortlisting and appointing applicants from the field generated by the recruitment activity. It usually starts by comparing the information contained in an application form or CV (curriculum vitae) against the criteria established in the person specification or competency profile. At this point, selection decisions are then taken about who will be rejected and who will be invited for further assessment. It follows from this that application forms or CVs are important tools in the selection process and the choice of either one or the other method is worthy of more consideration than it is often accorded. Thus the first section below explores these issues. Thereafter, a range of tools are available for further assessment. The most important are interviewing, psychometric testing and assessment centres and these will also be considered below. Other methods available include 'biodata' (the study of biographical data about applicants to predict future performance) and graphology (the study and interpretation of an applicant's handwriting as a predictor of future performance) but are rarely used according to the CIPD's 1999 recruitment survey and will not be considered here.

From a psychometric perspective, the key issue when choosing a selection method is concerned with its 'validity': the extent to which the selection method is a valid measure of the candidate's capabilities in relation to the criteria for effective performance documented in person specifications or competency profiles. If a selection method were to be 100% valid, it would be a perfect predictor of future performance. As indicated in Table 3.1, no selection tool provides a perfect prediction, but some tools have been found by research to have been more valid predictors than others. It has to be accepted that, with the tools currently available, predicting who will or will not prove successful in the job and making a decision about which candidate will be selected for a post continues to carry risks and uncertainties, but as indicated below, there are tools available which help to reduce these risks. In Table 3.1, a perfect predictor would have a validity coefficient of 1.0 and a chance predictor, one which has no predictive value other than selecting the best fitted candidate by chance, has a validity coefficient of 0 (Corbridge and Pilbeam, 1998: 102).

Assessment centres designed for in-house use for identifying employees with promotion potential have proved to be highly valid as predictors of future performance. More will be said below about their counterparts for external recruitment and selection, but suffice it to say here that the high validity of these internal assessment centres can in part be explained by the make-up of the group of

Table 3.1 Predictive capability of selection tools

1.0	**Perfect prediction**
0.9	
0.8	
0.7	Assessment centres for development/promotability
0.6	Skilful and structured interviews
0.5	Work sampling
	Ability tests
0.4	Assessment centres for recruitment and selection
	Personality assessment
0.3	Traditional unstructured interviews
0.2	
0.1	References
0	**Chance prediction**:
	Graphology
	Astrology

people under assessment. Their make-up is highly selective and consists of people who have already demonstrated both capability and potential, often over a period of years, through their work performance. When applied to new recruits, assessment centres offer lower but still respectable levels of validity with a coefficient of 0.4.

Significantly, validity coefficients of the order of 0.6 have been achieved through the use of skilful and structured interviews, compared with a figure of half when the traditional, unstructured interview is used. In effect this means that 60% of candidates selected through structured interviewing prove to be effective in their jobs, compared with 30% using unstructured techniques. Though not a perfect predictor, the structured interview offers scope for organisations to improve considerably the validity of interview decisions. Both the unstructured and structured techniques will be considered further below.

The use of psychometric testing, for example ability or aptitude and personality tests, also generates respectable levels of validity. References, on the other hand, have not proved very effective in predicting performance. Rarely used techniques such as astrology or graphology have not been found to have any validity as predictors of future performance and thus if someone were selected on the basis of their findings, any connection between these and future success in a job would be pure chance.

Sifting and shortlisting

Sifting and shortlisting take place in relation to the selection criteria established in the person specification or competency profile and require that the details provided by candidates are systematically reviewed and compared against the established criteria. It is vital, therefore, that these documents are adequate for this purpose. Person specifications that consist of vaguely worded requirements – 'good interpersonal skills', 'good communication skills', 'working knowledge of IT', etc. – will generally not provide adequate yardsticks against which to assess candidates. Ideally, they should be framed in precise terms of what a competent applicant should be able to do, so that specific questions can be asked at interview about their experience of doing these things. As noted earlier, person specifications should specify these requirements under a range of predefined attributes and need to reflect both generic qualities and the specific 'technical' skills and knowledge implied by the job description. It is vital that candidates are assessed in relation to both. Without an appropriate balance, it would be possible to select an engineer who has excellent interpersonal, team leading and communications skills, but who is not proficient in performing the technical skills required in the role. Equally, from an opposite perspective, it would be possible to select an engineer who is technically proficient, but lacks the generic qualities or attributes to lead and motivate a team. The same point may be made about the use of competency frameworks and it is important that these include both the generic and technical competencies required for performing the role. For sifting and shortlisting purposes, a simple scoring system can be devised which rates candidates according to whether they appear to meet, nearly meet or fail to meet both essential and desirable requirements. Because of the risks of error and bias, the sifting process should ideally be carried out by more than one person, typically the line manager filling a vacancy and the human resource specialist.

The use of application forms and CVs in sifting and shortlisting

Given the emphasis on sifting and shortlisting against carefully defined criteria, a process which can be prone to error, the method of gathering information from candidates is of vital importance. For many reasons, a well-designed application form will prove superior to a CV for the following reasons (Corbridge and Pilbeam, 1998; Roberts, 1997; Taylor, 1998; Torrington and Hall, 1998).

First, it can and should be designed to gather information specific to the selection criteria and attributes contained in the person specification or competency framework and should not be seen simply as a pro forma for gathering random items of data needed for an employment record. If the criteria established are the basis on which effective performers will be assessed and selection decisions taken, candidates must be given an opportunity to provide evidence against each of the criteria in the application form. In this way, the employer effectively sets an agenda for what is important and a number have already adopted a 'competency-based application form' which requires applicants to give specific examples of how they have met specified competency requirements in their current or previous roles (IRS, 1994). By contrast, CVs do not automatically do this since they consist of the information selected by the applicant which may, but more likely may not, provide the specific evidence required against all the criteria – in effect, the candidate has set the agenda of what is important.

Secondly, application forms are standardised. Not only are all applicants required to provide the same information, which aids equality of treatment based on the facts presented, but the presentation of the information will be consistent within each application form, making the comparison of the information during sifting and shortlisting easier and less prone to error. CVs will not provide the same degree of standardisation and make sifting and shortlisting more difficult, less consistent and more prone to error.

Thirdly, application forms facilitate the process of equal opportunities monitoring as recommended by the various codes of practice since they can be so designed as to remove from consideration during sifting and shortlisting any information which might be a source of illegal discrimination. Such information usually includes gender/title, ethnic origin and disability and increasingly other information such as age or religion. For the purposes of monitoring applicants, this information will be recorded either on a 'tear-off' slip or on a separate form. By implication, CVs cannot provide these facilities. Either the information is not provided and therefore cannot be monitored or it is provided and can be a potential source of illegal discrimination in sifting and shortlisting.

Fourthly, application forms can be used to obtain candidates' signatures as to the truth of the information provided (e.g. about qualifications, health record, criminal record, etc.) and help to protect the employer's position should evidence arise in future as to the truth or reliability of the information given. Such undertakings do not by implication form part of the content of CVs, though undertakings could be sought as part of the offer of employment (but in practice rarely are).

Many employers do make use of CVs, as evidenced by the survey data from the CIPD's recruitment survey noted on p. 97, and it is probable that they are preferred by candidates seeking employment. They have the benefit of speed, an important consideration when recruiting in a tight labour market. They will generally be preferred by candidates, especially those who have multiple job applications running concurrently, for whom the repeated filling of application forms may act as a deterrent to pursuing a vacancy. They are said to be useful in selection as a sample of a candidate's work, though whether this will always be so in practice must be open to doubt. It is recognised that the use of CVs is entrenched in the culture of certain sectors, particularly the IT sector where agencies are widely used and speed is of the essence and skills are in high demand but short supply. From the perspective of criteria-based selection aimed at making the process more effective and from the perspective of legal compliance, a well designed application form is the superior tool.

The use of telephone screening in sifting and shortlisting

The use of telephone screening in sifting and shortlisting is used by 18% of employers according to the CIPD's 1999 survey of recruitment and selection practices and its use appears to have increased in popularity in recent years. The use of telephone screening is particularly appropriate where an ability to perform competently on the telephone is central to the role to be filled, for example in telesales or telemarketing, help or advice line work, work involving customer orders, queries or complaints, etc.

The usual procedure is that an advertisement informs candidates of the number to be called in order to pursue a vacancy and sometimes the hours in which calls will be received are specified (for example, in the evening to avoid blocking lines during normal business hours). Calls are then normally handled by trained operators who have been briefed about the questions to be asked. Some approaches to telephone screening also incorporate screen-based computerised systems which require the operator to complete enquirer details, ask questions listed on the screen which are often based on 'yes or no' or short factual responses and record the results or rate the candidate according to a simple, screen-based scoring system. Questions asked normally relate to the essential requirements of the role, the absence of which would make it difficult for the incumbant to perform effectively, and the operator is also required to assess the telephone skills of the caller. Depending on the results obtained and following standardised instructions about how to proceed, the operator may then be empowered to generate an application form which will take the candidate to the next stage of the sifting process or a rejection letter. In the latter case, it is unusual for a rejection to be notified immediately at the end of the call (Roberts, 1997).

As an alternative, it is also possible for telephone screening to be carried out directly by staff in the personnel function without automated aids, but prior consideration needs to be given to the resources available to perform these additional duties, especially if there is a high response rate.

Telephone screening has the advantage that it is speedier than using the postal system and provides an effective way of assessing telephone skills which cannot readily be assessed through interviews or other means. It also has potential for reducing the administrative costs of processing high volumes of applications by conventional means. However, the use of telephone screening also carries significant costs where special software needs to purchased and adapted to the organisation's needs in addition to the cost of training the operators.

Selection interviewing

While interviews are almost universally used to select candidates – it is extremely rare, though not entirely unknown, for organisations to make an appointment without one – research has shown that the success rate of traditional interviews have a much higher chance of picking a less well fitted candidate than picking the one best fitted. The likelihood of getting the decision right, as discussed in the context of validity above, is about three times in ten, the corollary being that in seven cases in ten we make the wrong decision. On the basis of such a low success rate, it seems remarkable that employers still place so much faith in interviews. Fortunately, we need to distinguish between 'traditional' interviews and some more recently emerging interview strategies which have been shown by research to improve considerably on the success rate of the 'traditional' interview and it is to these that we shall turn below.

Inevitably, a question arises as to why interviews have proved to be such poor predictors of successful future performance, with all the implications that this has for the costs and future effectiveness of organisations. The reasons for this will become evident from the discussion of question strategies below, but the problems stem from the long recognised sources of bias in interpersonal perception. When making judgements about others, it is difficult to separate our own views with their inherent but often unconscious biases and prejudices; we stereoytpe in order to make sense of a complex world around us; we tend to like those who are like ourselves or like the things we like and vice versa. These latter problems are referred to as the 'halo' effect – being unduly influenced in favour of a candidate by one characteristic, such as the discovery of a mutual passion for golf, during an interview – that biases objective judgement. Its corollary is the 'horns' effect – some interest or characteristic of the candidate of which we disapprove – that is given undue weight against the candidate. The essential difficulty is remaining objective in our assessments of people and making judgements on the basis of the facts before us (Taylor, 1998). Many years ago, this was aptly demonstrated in some research into interviewer behaviour which identified that interviewers tend to make up their minds about the suitability of a candidate after an initial impression has been formed and within the first few minutes of an interview. Subconsciously, the remainder of the interview is spent confirming these first impressions (Torrington and Hall, 1998).

A number of key considerations arise when planning and conducting selection interviews. These are as follows and each will be considered in turn below:

- *Interview type.* How many interviewers should be used and how many interviews should be held?

- *Interview strategies.* What overall strategies or approaches are available when planning interviews?

- *Interview structure.* What are the conventional structures used in interviews?

- *Question strategies.* What questions should be asked?

- *Question techniques.* What question techniques are available for encouraging candidate response, getting below the surface to underlying issues and ensuring that clear information is obtained?

- *Other techniques and strategies for effective interviewing.*

Interview types

When planning interviews, there are three options concerning the number of interviewers to be used (Torrington and Hall, 1998). First, interviews may be 'one to ones', one interviewer and one interviewee. Second, they may be 'two to ones' or 'tandem' interviews. Thirdly, they may consist of panels of three or more interviewers and one interviewee. More rarely, they may be 'group' interviews, consisting of two or more interviewers and two or more interviewees. A further issue to consider when planning interviews is how many to hold: a single interview after which a selection decision is made or successive (or 'sequential') interviews, the use of more than one interview before making the final decision. Each has their advantages and disadvantages and the final decision needs to be made after weighing these.

One-to-one interviews

From many perspectives, one-to-one interviews have many advantages over the alternatives. They enable the interviewee to be more relaxed than when there is more than one interviewer and, in consequence, the interviewee is less likely to be defensive and more likely to be open about their strengths and weaknesses. A skilful interviewer is better able to build rapport with the candidate, gain their confidence and trust and create an environment of free and frank discussion. Such an environment enables the one-to-one interview to get below the surface and, in principle at least, obtain a deeper understanding of the attributes of the candidate. It also has the benefit that it saves on management time, particularly in comparison with a panel interview. To achieve this ideal, however, the one-to-one must be conducted by a skilful interviewer, but even in this case there remains the problem of personal bias on the part of the interviewer which can distort objective judgement. Thus the reliance on the judgement of one person in making selection decisions is a major disadvantage of the one-to-one. Where organisations have active policies on equal opportunities and wish to ensure compliance with non-discrimination law and the associated official codes of practice, the risks of bias as a result of placing these decisions in the hands of one person have made the one-to-one interview undesirable. A further practical problem with one-to-one interviews is that they often need to be used sequentially. A typical use of the one-to-one is to carry out an initial screening, with the interview being conducted by a personnel specialist or by an employee at supervisor level. Having been successful at the screening stage, an applicant is invited back for a further interview with a more senior person. In some instances, especially where the appointment is a senior one, further successive one-to-ones are held before a decision is made. This is not only time-consuming for both the candidate and the organisation, but often tedious for the candidate who may be asked the same questions over and over again.

Panel interviews

A panel interview – an interview with at least three interviewers, but sometimes many more – is the diametric opposite of the one-to-one, with opposing advantages and disadvantages. It is more formal and less relaxing for candidates and candidates will tend to be more defensive and less open or forthcoming with information. The creation of rapport is much more difficult and the scope for getting below the surface potentially more limited. It also requires careful planning so that each interviewer knows in advance what their role will be – who will ask which question and how follow-up questions will be handled. It also needs careful prior planning to ensure that all the interviewers who need to attend are available on the day. Its main advantages relate to their reduced bias and subjectivity because the decision-making is in the hands of a number of people and would thus be preferred where equal opportunities considerations are given high priority. Usually, though not exclusively, a single panel interview is held with each candidate after which a decision is made. This has the benefit that all those who need to be a party to the decision are present, the time of candidates is saved and the need to ask the same questions again is avoided.

Two-to-one interviews

The two-to-one interview seeks to achieve a compromise between the alternatives of the one-to-one and the panel. Survey evidence of interviewing practice indicates that the public sector prefers the panel interview and the private sector the two-to-one. While panels have long been the preference of the public sector, the two-to-one has replaced the private sector's previous preference for one-to-ones except in the case of more junior appointments. Thus the choice between panels and two-to-ones has become as much an issue of custom and the differing cultures of decision-making between the public and the private sectors.

Interview strategies

Torrington and Hall (1991, 1998) suggest that there are four possible strategies or approaches to the conduct of a selection interview.

The 'frank and friendly' strategy

This is best achieved through the use of one-to-one interviews and possibly also two-to-ones, but would rarely be achievable through the use of panels.

The main emphasis is on relaxing the candidate in order to encourage him or her to speak freely. The strategy is also likely to be used in conjunction with a 'biographical' question strategy which, as discussed below, encourages the candidate to talk freely about themselves and their current and past work experience.

Its main disadvantage is that unless it is conducted by a skilful interviewer it may descend into an informal chat and fail to get below the surface and reveal in-depth information about the candidate. It also suffers from the inherent shortcomings of unstructured interviews and 'biographical' question strategies about which more will be said later.

While it usually succeeds in creating a positive impression of the organisation, this type of strategy may be described as the 'traditional unstructured' interview which, as noted, results in low levels of validity in terms of successfully predicting who will be effective in the job if selected.

The structured interview strategy

In contrast to the strategy noted above, which encourages candidates to talk freely about themselves and their past work experience, the structured approach involves the careful preparation of questions in advance which will be asked of all candidates. The questions themselves will all be derived from the criteria contained in the person specification or competency profile and will usually involve the use of what have been termed 'behavioural' or 'situational' questions, about which more will be said in the section on question strategies below.

Suffice it to say here that the research into the validity of selection interviews (Janz et al., 1986; Latham, 1989), as discussed earlier, has established that structured interviews have proved far more effective as predictors of future performance than their traditional, unstructured counterparts and therefore have considerable potential for organisations wishing to improve the effectiveness of their current interview practices.

The 'stress' strategy

Though probably not widely used, a stress strategy involves the creation of a stressful environment in an interview in order to assess a candidate's coping abilities and responses. The aim is to simulate how the candidate might respond to stressors in a real working environment. This is usually simulated by adopting an aggressive stance towards candidates, provoking responses by intentionally disagreeing with what candidates have said or using eccentric behaviour (such as getting up and walking around or staring out of the window during the interview).

Though the approach may appeal to some interviewers and may indeed help to assess some qualities in the candidate such as assertiveness, it has a number of serious drawbacks. Interviews should as a subsidiary aim endeavour to leave the candidate with a favourable impression of the organisation and a feeling that they were fairly treated, even where they have been unsuccessful. More fundamentally, however, there are questions about whether the types of behaviour displayed by the interviewer actually simulate real events which would be likely to occur in the job. If, for example, dealing with angry customers is occasionally part of the job, there are more realistic ways of simulating how the candidate would deal with them. It would, for example, be possible to ask a candidate about how they have dealt with an angry customer in the past or ask how they would do so if they had not had such an experience. It would also be possible to simulate such a situation by designing an exercise contained in an assessment centre. Thus, a stress strategy, while an available option, is probably not one that many organisations would wish to use.

The 'sweet and sour' strategy

This strategy involves two interviewers, one adopting an approach similar to the 'frank and friendly' strategy and the other an approach akin to that which might be adopted in the 'stress' strategy. The aim of the first interviewer is to create rapport and a relaxed environment in which the candidate is encouraged to talk freely and openly. The second interviewer, by contrast, adopts a more aggressive stance and the interview progresses with the candidate being exposed first to the one for a period and then to the other.

It is said that the candidate will eventually resist the pressure put on them by the stress interviewer and that they will overcompensate by opening up to the friendlier interviewer and thus reveal the truth about themselves. The use of this practice is rare but not unheard of, but its use suffers from the same shortcomings as the stress interview and these make it generally undesirable.

Interview structure

Interview structures have three parts: an opening, a middle and a close (Torrington and Hall, 1998). The opening is short, but performs important functions in terms of the effectiveness of the interview as a whole. Its purpose is to welcome the candidate, put them at their ease (for example, by asking them about their journey) and remind them briefly of the post for which they have applied. It is important that the interviewer does not delay getting into their questioning for long since most interviewees will be nervous at this point and encouraging them to talk helps them to relax and get into their stride. It is important to give information about the job and the organisation, but this may best be done later in the interview. If too much information is given at the start of the interview, it is unlikely that the interviewee is ready to absorb much until they have relaxed and are ready to listen.

The middle represents the body of the interview and consists of the questions put by the interviewer and the responses of the interviewee. There is a considerable number of techniques which need to be deployed here and these will be considered under the sections below on question strategies and other techniques for conducting effective interviews. When the interviewer is satisfied that they have asked all the questions necessary to assess the suitability of the candidate, it is then appropriate to give the candidate information about the job, the salary, the benefits, the opportunities (e.g. training, development, promotion, etc.) and the organisation and give the candidate ample time to ask further questions.

Having checked with the candidate that they have no further questions, the time has arrived to close the interview and it is important that the interviewer remembers that they have to initiate this by thanking the candidate for their responses and telling them what happens next. This needs to include how the outcome of the interview will be communicated to the candidate and in what timescale. If subsequently there are any changes to these, in particular any changes in the timescales envisaged, it is courteous to notify the candidate about this when any changes have become apparent.

Question strategies

These lie at the heart of effective interviewing and also at the heart of the issue of validity discussed earlier. The two broad strategies available are unstructured biographical questions or a structured, criteria-based approach using behavioural or situational questions (Roberts, 1997). Each of these will be considered in turn.

Unstructured biographical question strategies

Unstructured biographical questioning represents the traditional approach to interviewing. It usually involves preparation by perusing the application form or CV to identify any issues which the interviewer wishes to raise (for example, any unexplained gaps in the candidate's employment history) and familiarisation with the candidate's current and previous roles. The interview is referred to as 'unstructured' because no set questions are written down in advance and 'biographical' because the candidate will be encouraged through the use of open questions (see 'question techniques' below) to talk freely and openly about their current and past roles and possibly also about other information given on the application form or CV, for example hobbies or interests. The strategy is usually the 'frank and friendly' approach described above.

One well-known and long established framework for the conduct of biographical interviews is the 'WASP' model. An explanation of the 'WASP' acronym is as follows:

- **W**elcome – the candidate is welcomed, thanked for coming, introduced to any others present and the structure of the interview is explained.

- **A**cquire information from the candidate by asking open, biographical questions which enable the candidate to explain their career in chronological order.

- **S**upply information about the job, the salary, the benefits and the organisation.

- **P**art by asking if the candidate has any further questions, tell the candidate about what happens next and when, thank them for attending and complete a candidate assessment after their departure.

The main benefits of the traditional, unstructured interview are that they enable the candidate to relax and offer an unpressurised environment in which the candidate is encouraged to talk about themselves and what they have done. For the interviewer, they offer flexibility to probe and follow up any aspect of what the candidate has said in relation to the vacancy in hand. The significant disadvantage is that the interview is driven more by what the candidate wishes to say in response to the open questions asked and this may or may not, depending on what the candidate's actual experience has been, provide specific evidence in relation to the requirements of the post. In order to correct this shortcoming, the interviewer may employ a 'semi-structured' approach in which they tick off those attributes on the person specification for which information has been provided and add specific questions about those areas for which no evidence has been given (Taylor, 1998). However, the basic problem of this approach remains: the interview has not been driven from the outset by the criteria for effective performance (established in the person specification or competency framework) against which each candidate needs to be assessed. The interview is more 'candidate-driven' than driven by the organisation's own agenda in terms of its criteria for effective performance. The result is that the traditional unstructured interview provides an imperfect means of matching candidates to the organisation's requirements, as indicated by the typical validity coefficient of 0.3 noted earlier, and increases the likelihood that the wrong decision will be made because each of the selection criteria have not been measured systematically.

Structured, criteria-based question strategies

Research during the 1980s has demonstrated that the use of structured interviews, based on pre-defined lists of questions asked of all candidates and derived from the person specification or competency profile, produce more valid results (Janz et al., 1986; Latham, 1989). Following a time lag between the dissemination of these research findings and their implementation in practice, more organisations are recognising the potential of this approach and have adopted the use of structured interviews. For this approach to be used, it is essential that the criteria for effective performance are established through person specifications or, increasingly today, competency profiles which survey evidence suggests are now used by between a third and a half of organisations (Armstrong and Baron, 1998; CIPD, 1999). Thus one or more of the techniques discussed in the section on job analysis above need to have been implemented. Structured interviewing starts from the premise that, having established the criteria for effective performance, they must be assessed by asking a specific question about each criterion in the interview. Thus careful preparation is required in which the questions to be asked are written down in advance of the interview.

The research has offered two approaches to the formation of the questions to be asked in structured, criteria-based interviews, both of which have been demonstrated to produce much higher validity than traditional biographical techniques. The first approach to the formation of these questions is the 'behavioural' strategy or more fully the 'Patterned Behaviour Description Interview' (Janz et al., 1986). Having identified the criteria to be measured, the behavioural question involves asking the candidate to relate a specific example from their past experience in relation to each performance criterion.

Given that truthfulness cannot be assumed in interviews, it has been argued that this approach is more likely to generate truthful answers on the grounds that candidates are being asked to relate real past events: their task is simply to recall them and time must be allowed by the interviewer for them to do so. The behavioural question is also based on the premise that past behaviour is likely to be repeated in the future and is therefore a good guide to how people will actually perform in a job.

Behavioural questions start with such openers as 'tell me about a time when...' or 'give me an example of an occasion when...' or 'tell me how you go about...' and the subject matter of the question may draw from the 'critical incidents' in the job identified through job analysis. Thus, if one of our criteria against which candidates will be assessed relates to 'effective team working', the behavioural question might be phrased as 'tell me about a time when you worked in a team'. If another is about planning work, the question might be 'tell me how you plan your week's work'. Because the questions are phrased in behavioural terms in that they specifically ask for examples of how candidates do things, they are designed to produce specific information about the candidate at work. In a way, they are aimed at generating samples of oral evidence of their work behaviour. It is vital, therefore, that the selection criteria include yardsticks of what the organisation sees as more effective or less effective behaviours when establishing the selection criteria against which candidates are being assessed. The task of assessment then involves rating the candidate's response on a simple rating scale according to how closely it matches the behaviours seen by the organisation as more or less effective. In a sense, this means that in a given organisational setting there will be 'right' or 'wrong' answers in that some candidates' responses will more closely correlate with the required behaviours than others.

The use of competencies provides a very useful framework for the application of this question technique since each competency is expressed in terms of performance criteria defined in behavioural terms. Either a competency will be defined in terms of what behaviour is required in order to perform competently or they will be defined in terms of gradated statements of competent behaviours.

An alternative strategy offered by the research is known as the 'situational' question (Latham, 1989). This employs a different technique for eliciting evidence of candidate performance. It involves putting to candidates scenarios about specific job-related situations which may arise, possibly based on the identification of 'critical incidents' during job analysis (Newell, 2000), as discussed earlier, or asking how candidates 'would go about' or 'would deal with' particular situations. As with behavioural questions considered above, each question needs to be designed in relation to the documented criteria for effective performance (the person specification or competency profile), including descriptors of the behaviours sought. In the same way as the behavioural question, answers are compared and rated against these descriptors, matching candidate response with the required behaviours.

The approach has been criticised on the grounds that such questions are 'hypothetical' and seek evidence not based on what candidates have actually done, but on what they say they would do which might not be what they actually would do in practice (Torrington and Hall, 1998). Another criticism is that situational questions may tend to generate 'textbook' answers which may or may not reflect what they would do in a real situation, i.e. knowing the 'theory' is not the same as putting it into practice (Taylor, 1998). Nevertheless, the use of situational questions has also been shown by the research to generate higher levels of validity than traditional biographical questions, on a par with the behavioural approach (Newell, 2000).

Questioning techniques

Beyond the issue of question strategies, there is also a range of questioning techniques which are relevant whichever strategy is to be used. They are essentially concerned with ways in which questions are formed to encourage the candidate to give information, to build an exchange of questions and answers which penetrate below the surface in order to provide precise information and help the interviewer clarify what has been said so that an accurate assessment of the candidate's abilities in relation to the criteria for the position can be made. These techniques are as follows (Torrington and Hall, 1991, 1998):

- *Open questions.* These are the mainstay of the selection interview and are designed to encourage the candidate to give information. They will nearly always be the first question asked each time the interviewer wishes to explore a given aspect of a candidate's experience. The behavioural and situational questions noted above were good examples of open questions: 'tell me about a time when...' or 'tell me how you would go about handling the following situation...' Other typical opening words in open questions include 'when', 'why', 'where', 'how' or 'tell me more about'.

- *Closed questions.* These tend to be used sparingly in interviews as they often invite the answer 'yes' or 'no', but can be useful for confirming specific facts or getting clarification.

- *Probes.* These types of questions lie at the heart of well-developed interview skills and are important for getting below the surface of an answer given to an open question. Probes, along with follow-up questions, help the interview develop into an in-depth exchange rather than being simply a series of questions each followed by a single answer. Asking probe questions following information given by a candidate in response to an open question requires active and attentive listening so as to pick up words, phrases or remarks made which have been glossed over by the candidate, but which if explored may reveal further information of significance.

- *Follow-up questions.* Similar to probes, the follow-up is an open question inviting a candidate to give more information about some aspect of their answer. Its usual purpose will be to explore some aspect in more detail in order to obtain more in-depth evidence in relation to the candidate's experience.

- *Direct questions.* While used sparingly, direct questions ask the candidate to provide some specific information about matters that the candidate has been unwilling to enlarge upon when requested to do so in a probe or follow-up question, for example 'exactly why did you leave that employment?'

- *Summary and re-run.* When a candidate has provided a lot of information in response to a question, some of it not entirely clear, the summary and re-run requires the interviewer to summarise their understanding of what has been said and check with the candidate that they have understood correctly the essential facts.

- *Leading questions.* A leading question is one that is phrased in such a way that the candidate is led to make a certain response and is a type of question to be avoided since the answer required of the candidate will have been strongly implied in the question. Effectively, it involves 'putting words' into the candidate's mouth and is a trap that less experienced interviewers can easily fall into.

- *Braking.* This is an important technique for keeping the interview to its allotted time schedule and politely stopping the candidate's flow of information once sufficient has been said in answer to a question put. Some candidates may be very forthcoming with information and go on to provide unnecessary detail or begin to repeat information already provided, in effect going round in circles. An important role of the interviewer is to keep control of the interview and move it on to the next question when sufficient information has been gathered. This requires polite interjection at the appropriate moment with such words as 'thank you for telling me about that, I fully understand what you have been saying and would like to ask you about something else', followed by the next question.

- *Evaluative questions.* Like leading questions, evaluative questions are phrased in such a way that implies disapproval of something that the candidate has done and are to be avoided, for example, 'why did you leave a promising career at organisation X for a job at Y?' This implies disapproval of this job move. Or, 'would I be right in saying that your job only involves administrative duties?' Here, the insertion of the word 'only' belittles the candidate. It is not the role of interviewer to make negative judgements about a candidate during an interview, unless techniques associated with the stress interview are being deployed. The role of the interviewer is to remain unbiased and neutral and to ask open questions without revealing personal opinions.

- *Multiple questions.* Questions which contain multiple sub-parts, such as 'why did you leave that job and take a job at company X, only to leave within three months', should be avoided. Candidates may either be confused or simply answer the part which they prefer. The general principle is that one issue should be asked about in an initial question and subsequent probes or follow-ups should be used to illuminate further details.

Other techniques for conducting effective interviews

A number of further techniques which need to be considered when planning and conducting effective interviews include the following.

Preparation

From what has been said, it will be evident that interviewing requires careful preparation. Where unstructured, biographical interviews are to be used, this requires the interviewer to be familiar with the job description and the person specification and to have studied the candidate's application form or CV and have considered any issues which they wish to raise from the information provided. For the structured interview, considerably more planning is required in order to determine in advance the schedule of questions which will be asked of all candidates by reference to the job description, person specification or competency profile. A number of organisations using structured interviews have compiled a standard list of questions to be asked, particularly where all interviews are based on or include questions designed to measure the organisation's competency framework. Where more than one interviewer is to be used, it is vital that preparation includes clarification of who will ask which questions, how will follow-up questions will be handled and how notes will be taken (Taylor, 1998; Torrington and Hall, 1998).

Planning

In addition to preparing questions, it is important that the timing of interviews is planned in advance, allowing sufficient and identical time for each interview, with time allowed after each for writing a summary and holding a brief discussion where more than one interviewer is involved. Some time for planned breaks should be included since interviewing candidates for a full day is tiring. It is also important that on the day of the interviews, the timetable is strictly adhered to in order to ensure that candidates are not kept waiting: this not only creates a poor impression on the candidate, but may also affect their performance in the interview (Roberts, 1997).

Environment

Getting the environment right for the interview helps candidates perform at their best. Interviews should not be conducted across a table, which acts as a barrier to effective communication, disrupts the creation of rapport and can cause defensiveness on the part of the candidate. The interview should be conducted in a neat and tidy environment and arrangements should be made so that there are no interruptions, either from telephone calls or from people entering and disrupting the proceedings (Torrington and Hall, 1998).

Taking notes

It is vital that some notes are taken of candidates' responses because it will not be easy to recall in any detail what has been said after the interview has ended, let alone at the end of a heavy day's interviewing (Roberts, 1997). Where unstructured interviewing is to be used, it is helpful to have a version of the person specification available, set out in such a way that notes can be entered alongside each of the requirements contained in it. Where structured interviewing is to be used, such a pro forma should contain the questions to be asked, with space alongside each to summarise replies. Under both methods, a simple scoring system may be incorporated on which the interviewer or interviewers rate the candidate in terms of exceeding, meeting or not meeting requirements. It is important that note-taking is done in such a way that it is unobtrusive and does not obviously interrupt proceedings and it is usually courteous to explain to the candidate that a few notes will be taken.

Manner and style

It is important that the interviewer takes time and adopts an unhurried approach. Interviewers should allow the candidate sufficient time to consider their replies and thus the use of silence is important. Interrupting a candidate should be avoided, unless it is necessary to bring their information giving to an end because sufficient has been heard. The interviewer should be attentive at all times and eye contact should be maintained throughout. The interviewer should also listen actively and closely to what is being said because it is often just a passing word or phrase that provides a cue for a probe or follow-up question.

Psychological testing

Psychological tests fall into two broad categories (Toplis et al., 1997): tests of aptitude or ability and tests (or more properly questionnaires) designed to profile personality. The former are concerned with measuring mental abilities in relation to the attributes required for effective performance in a role and the latter are concerned with profiling personality in relation to some pre-defined profile seen as appropriate for effective performance in a role. It is important to note that psychological testing does not occur in a vacuum, but must be used specifically to measure criteria identified as relevant to effective performance. Thus the role of tests is to measure criteria identified in job analysis.

Tests of ability or aptitude

This group of tests falls into three sub-categories (Toplis et al., 1997):

- *Tests of achievement or attainment.* These are practical tests that measure performance on the basis of observing and measuring candidates performing a sample of the work. A typical test of this type would be a typing test which measures how many words can be typed in a specified period and to what degree of accuracy.

- *Tests of general intelligence.* These usually contain sub-elements which measure verbal, numerical and diagrammatic components that are said to make up general intelligence. There has been something of a debate about the links between intelligence and job performance and survey evidence suggests that intelligence tests are not widely used as tools of selection. They might, however, be appropriate for school leaver recruitment as an additional measure of capability beyond relying on GCSE results alone.

- *Aptitude tests.* These represent a large and important category of tests which are widely used for selection purposes. Their advantage over the test of attainment, noted above, is that many jobs do not readily lend themselves to practical testing because of the range or complexity of tasks performed and various aptitude tests, involving pencil and paper, can be used to identify the special or underlying aptitudes relevant for effective performance. Some of these tests are designed to assess the attributes required for a particular type of occupation, for example clerical accuracy, selling ability, language ability, computer aptitude, mechanical aptitude, etc. Alternatively, a range of different tests may be used, each designed to measure a different component which is central to effective job performance. Having identified from job analysis the key attributes or competencies required in a role, e.g. written communications skills, problem-solving skills, creativity, etc., it is possible to identify tests which measure these attributes.

Personality questionnaires

The use of personality questionnaires for selection is based on the proposition that jobs can be analysed in terms of a personality profile which correlates with success. Most personality questionnaires are built around what are known as the 'Big 5' personality factors (Roberts, 1997):

- extroversion–introversion

- emotional stability

- agreeableness

- conscientiousness

- openness to experience.

There are two broad approaches to the identification of a profile which correlates with success. One is to administer a number of personality tests to the current population of employees occupying the posts for which testing will be introduced. Independent assessments then need to be obtained which categorise these employees as either better performers or less effective performers, using such measures as appraisal ratings, promotions, salary progression or managers' ratings. From this can be identified the profiles of the more effective and less effective performers and these can then be used as the basis of comparison when selecting or rejecting candidates. The problem with this method is that it is time-consuming and may be based on samples which are too small to provide statistically significant results. A second and apparently more used approach is to rely on the occupational profiles provided by the test suppliers, based on research with a large sample of candidates. Selection then becomes an issue of determining the profile of each applicant and matching it against the occupational profile for the role.

The leading personality test in use in the UK is the 'Occupational Personality Questionnaire (OPQ)' from Saville and Holdworth, but others in use include Cattell's 16 Personality Factor questionnaire (16PF), the Myers-Briggs Type Indicator, the Californian Psychological Inventory and the Thomas International Personality Profile (Toplis et al., 1997).

Implementing psychological tests

Psychological tests may only be purchased, administered and interpreted by those qualified by attendance on specific training courses to do so. Thus organisations wishing to implement them have either to seek the services of a consultant psychologist or put staff through the required training, unless they already have qualified staff. These costs can be considerable, but need to be weighed against the costs of making incorrect selection decisions. In addition to the significant costs of training staff, there are also costs associated with licensing fees for the use of tests, charges for each item of test material used, the time of staff involved in test administration and interpretation and the costs of facilities for carrying out the testing. The general qualifications for using tests are the Level A and Level B courses run under the auspices of the British Psychological Society: Level A qualifies users in administering, scoring and interpreting ability or aptitude tests and Level B provides the equivalent for personality tests. As an alternative, potential test buyers may attend the specific training courses run by the major test suppliers. These may be offered at two levels: qualification as a test administrator and further training to qualify as a test interpreter (Toplis et al., 1997).

Issues in the implementation of testing

There are three general issues to consider when purchasing tests and information needs to be sought from suppliers about these before making any decision to buy. First, data needs to be sought to assure a purchaser that the tests are 'valid', i.e. they measure the characteristics that they purport to measure. If they are not, then the whole exercise will be a waste of time and unnecessary expense. Reputable test suppliers will have conducted validation research on large samples of the population and will also have conducted follow-up studies to check that the attributes demonstrated in the test are, to an acceptable level, also demonstrated in practice. Perfect prediction would yield a coefficient of validity of 1, but as a rule tests generate lower levels of validity. According to Smith and Robertson (1993), a coefficient of validity of 0.5 or above would be excellent, 0.4 to 0.49 good, 0.3 to 0.39 acceptable and below 0.3 poor. An important and related issue when selecting tests is 'culture fairness' and the extent to which they fairly assess the characteristics and attributes of all candidates, irrespective of gender and ethnic or cultural background. Tests which do not do this could leave the employer open to claims of indirect discrimination. Thus, it is important to establish that the supplier has extended validation research to test for and eliminate any potential sources of illegal bias.

A second issue for the test buyer is to satisfy themselves in relation to test 'reliability', that is the extent to which the test produces consistent results, since clearly tests which do not cannot be relied upon for selection purposes. Testing for reliability is carried out by reputable test suppliers, either by retesting candidates using the same test or by testing the performance of candidates using a parallel test during test construction. According to Toplis et al. (1997), a coefficient of reliability of 0.75 for ability tests and 0.65 for personality tests would be considered acceptable and information about the reliability achieved by the supplier during test construction should be sought.

A third issue to consider when buying tests is the availability of 'norms'. Norms are presented in tables showing the performance of a population who have undertaken the test in terms of a statistical distribution and provide yardsticks to users for interpreting results. The results of ability tests are usually given in the form of a raw score, but the meaning of a score can only be interpreted in relation to the scores obtained by a significant sample of people: a score of 65 in a test with a possible range of scores from 0 to 90 has no significance of itself. If, however, the norms table shows that this score is at the seventieth percentile, this places the candidate above 70% of those tested. Norms tables should also contain some breakdown of statistics according to different characteristics of the populations tested so that valid comparisons can be made between these and the scores of candidates taking the test, and the points made about 'culture fairness' above also apply. Norms tables are also relevant when interpreting the results of personality questionnaires and again the same principles about the background of the populations tested apply.

Extent of use of psychological tests

The use of psychological or psychometric testing for selection purposes has grown markedly in recent years. Surveys by Aston University showed that 30% of organisations used aptitude or ability tests and 35% personality questionnaires in 1985, while these figures had risen to 65% and 75% by 1995 (*People Management*, August 1996). A more recent survey (CIPD, 1999) found a similar level of usage of ability or aptitude tests (61% of respondents), but found a lower figure than in the Aston 1995 survey using personality tests (43% of respondents). The overall picture nevertheless suggests that the use of psychological testing has enjoyed considerable growth, especially in relation to the use of ability or aptitude tests. The reasons are not hard to surmise. As indicated in the table on p. 53, along with structured interviewing, the use of ability tests and personality questionnaires offers considerable potential for raising the predictive validity of the selection process and improves the chances of making a more effective decision.

Assessment centres

Assessment centres have grown considerably in popularity in the UK in recent years (CIPD, 1999) and involve the use of multiple selection tools. As noted earlier, the reasons for their growth relate to the opportunities potentially available through the use of assessment centres for enhancing the validity of selection decisions. In addition to interviewing and the use of psychometric tests, already considered, the assessment centre also incorporates a range of exercises designed to observe candidates' work behaviours in a simulated work context. The remainder of this section will be concerned with this latter aspect. It needs to be stressed that the term 'assessment centre' does not refer to a place where prospective candidates may be sent, but to the battery of exercises devised by employers to aid the selection decision (Woodruffe, 2000).

Assessment centres are usually held in suites of hotel rooms hired by employers for the purpose, though such places as company training centres may also be used. Assessment centres are not cheap to design and administer: much management time will be involved in their design and administration, in addition to the costs of any facilities hired in order to run them. Key issues in the design of assessment centres are as follows and each of these will be considered in turn (Roberts, 1997):

- defining the criteria for assessment;

- designing the exercises;

- piloting and validating the exercises in relation to the criteria to be assessed;

- briefing and training managers as assessors and interpreting results.

Defining criteria for assessment

As with the use of structured interviewing and psychological tests, the starting point for identifying the criteria for assessment is job analysis from which have been derived person specifications or competency profiles. In effect, therefore, assessment centres are concerned with providing additional evidence about candidate performance and potential in relation to the criteria identified as in the structured interview and the psychological test, but do it by work simulation exercises. Information gleaned in job analysis about 'critical incidents' can be useful guides to the design of exercises since they can be built into the simulations. Criteria for assessment might include oral and written communication, leadership, teamworking styles, planning and organising, delegation, judgement, creativity, etc., and it is important that job analysis has provided descriptions of what behaviours have been identified as more effective or less effective as yardsticks against which to assess the behaviours displayed by candidates. Competency frameworks, for example, provide such guidelines. Having identified what criteria are to be measured, the next task is to establish a range of exercises which provide opportunities for candidates to demonstrate the competencies under assessment in a simulated environment.

Designing the exercises

Woodruffe (2000) emphasises the importance of obtaining management commitment to the use of assessment centres through their full involvement in planning and designing the exercises. Project personnel are likely to include a coordinator, a steering group of senior managers to oversee the project and a project team of line managers responsible for the detailed design work. Organisations might also make use of a consultant, particularly where there is a lack of experience in designing assessment centres. It is also important that there are measurable and valid criteria in place around which to build exercises, but where there are not or where the current framework is inadequate, job analysis (as described earlier) will be required prior to the design of the exercises.

When designing exercises, it is useful to create a matrix or grid which shows the range of competencies being measured and the exercises which will measure them (Fletcher, 1997). It is usual that each exercise attempts to measure more than one competency and also that each competency is measured at least twice in different exercises. This enables candidates who were unable to adequately demonstrate their competency in one exercise to have at least one further chance to do so in another.

The following are examples of typical exercises included in assessment centres (Cook, 1993; Smith and Robertson, 1993; Taylor, 1998; Woodruffe, 2000).

In-tray exercises

In-tray exercises involve the compilation of a pile of letters, memos, notes and other correspondence containing information about the type of problems which a job holder might encounter when performing the role for which they are applying and will contain information designed to measure certain specific competencies. The number of items included in the collection of material can range from 20 to 30 and they will also be preceded by a sheet of background information about the organisation and the position occupied for the purpose of the exercise.

A typical opening scenario is that the incumbant has just returned from a two-week holiday and has been confronted with the pile of paper on their return to the office on a Monday morning. The exercise will be timed and can last from an hour to much longer and will be carried out to a specific brief. A typical brief might be to identify and prioritise the most urgent matters to be dealt with directly in, say, the first hour of the morning or to organise all the material in terms of urgency. The brief might also ask the candidate to say which items would be delegated and which would be handled directly.

The types of competency measured by in-tray exercises include planning and organising, breadth of business awareness, incisiveness, ability to delegate, problem-solving, decisiveness, etc. It is vital when designing the exercise that decisions have been taken in advance about what are seen as the most appropriate responses and that the candidate is assessed in the light of these. Candidates are usually asked to document their decisions and to give explanations for them. These may also be followed up in an interview which explores with the candidates the reasons underlying their decisions.

Group exercises

A variety of approaches are available around the general theme of having candidates working in groups. One approach is to provide a group of candidates with a written brief which sets out a problem to be solved. The problem should realistically reflect a situation which could occur in their role. An 'ideal' solution should be determined and reasons why other possible solutions would be less than optimum also need to have been considered. Another approach is to create a simulated exercise by getting a group of candidates to complete a practical task, such as building something out of a range of materials provided.

The types of competencies being measured in these types of group exercises include teamworking styles, communication skills, interpersonal skills, problem-solving ability, influencing skills, negotiating skills, etc. The performance of the exercise is observed and the roles taken on by participants noted, including the roles adopted by those who influence the group towards more effective or less effective outcomes.

An alternative approach is to assign roles to individuals in the group by giving each a specific brief and observe how the candidate deploys the skills necessary to argue their brief. A third variant is to set up the group exercise in the form of a debate or a negotiating exercise and observe the various roles assumed by the participants.

One-to-one role plays

In these exercises, each member of the observation staff takes on a specific brief to play a part, such as an angry customer, and the way the candidate handles the situation is observed. Such an exercise enables candidates to demonstrate competency in such areas as working under pressure, communication skills, ability to marshal arguments, negotiating skills, problem-solving, decisiveness, clarity of thought, etc.

Presentations

These are often used in assessment centres and a variety of different approaches is available. One approach is to ask the candidate to prepare a ten-minute presentation in advance, either on a topic of their own choosing or to a brief provided. Another is to provide a brief on the day and allow a short period for preparation. A third is to give a brief on the day and ask the candidate to give an instant presentation. As well as assessing candidates' communication and presentation skills, such exercises can assess their ability to master a brief quickly and can also be used to assess the candidate's knowledge in an area relevant to the post applied for.

Written exercises

A variety of approaches is available around the theme of a written exercise. One approach is to give the candidate a brief based on a problem or real situation that might be encountered in the job applied for. This might include marshalling arguments and giving a proposed solution with reasons. Another might involve writing a reply to a letter or memo setting out a reply to some problem posed. Another might involve writing a precis using a maximum number of words within a limited time period summarising the critical issues from a longer brief provided.

As well as assessing written communication skills, such exercises may also assess such competencies as problem-solving, business awareness, incisiveness, analytical abilities, etc. As with all assessment centre exercises, it will be necessary to determine in advance what competencies are being measured and how candidates' written responses are to be assessed against these criteria.

Designing assessment centres also requires that detailed briefs be prepared for observers, usually line managers, in order to help ensure that all assessors are working consistently and to the same criteria. Marking sheets need to be prepared which set out the behaviour sought or, as in the case of many competency frameworks, a range of behaviours reflecting competency descriptors (e.g. from not competent, to competent, to highly competent).

Piloting assessment centre exercises

Having devised the range of exercises to be deployed in an assessment centre, there are many sound reasons why the exercise should be put through a pilot or trial run before live implementation. In addition to giving observers an opportunity to become familiar with the exercises and their roles and testing the time taken in practice to run them, there is a vital question about validity. Do the exercises actually measure the qualities in candidates which they are intended to measure? At present, the exercises might look valid, but given the high cost of assessment and the weight being placed on selection decisions as a result of candidate performance in them, it is vital that the validity of the exercises is checked. It is not unheard of for an employer to make selection decisions following an assessment centre only to find in subsequent assessment, for example in performance appraisal, that the candidates selected actually perform weakly in areas identified as strengths in assessment centre exercises.

One approach to the validation of assessment centre exercises is to run them in pilot mode with a group of current employees who are similar to the population of applicants to be assessed. For example, if graduate trainees are to be selected through the assessment centre, the exercises can be piloted using last year's entrants or, if insufficient, the entrants over the last two or three years. This enables assessors to practise observation and scoring and to discuss and iron out any difficulties in a post assessment centre conference. More importantly from the perspective of validation, the assessment of the performance of the pilot candidates against each of the criteria being measured needs to be compared with independent assessments of their actual performance in the workplace. Such assessments may come from recent performance appraisals or the assessment of managers or supervisors. Where reasonable correlations are found between performance in a given exercise and actual performance in the job, there can be reasonable expectation that the exercise provides a valid measure of the performance criteria simulated. Where no such correlation is found, the exercise needs to be either withdrawn or modified and another successfully piloted before use for live selection purposes.

Planning and conducting the assessment centre

Having assembled and validated the exercises, it is important that observers are thoroughly trained and briefed about their roles. Since observation requires considerable concentration, it is usual to have one observer per candidate or one observer per two candidates at most. Facilities need to be booked for the assessment centre which typically lasts one or two days. Programmes and timetables need to be prepared and sent to candidates, including instructions about any preparation that they need to do in advance. All the materials for the day also need to be prepared and available (Woodruffe, 2000).

The sessions will usually be chaired by an appointed member of the management team and the day will normally start with a briefing of the candidates on what is to happen, where and when. After each round of exercises, observers' assessment forms will be passed to the chair. Following the completion of all the exercises, the chair and observers hold a meeting to discuss the performance of each of the candidates in turn and reach their decisions. It is generally the practice that all candidates, whether selected or not, are given feedback on their performance. For those selected, the information about their performance, for example areas requiring further development, can then be discussed as part of their personal development plans (Woodruffe, 2000).

Selection methods in practice

The CIPD's recruitment survey (1999) identified the frequency of use of various selection practices in relation to managerial, professional and skilled manual posts and its overall findings were as follows:

Interviews	100%
Application forms	82%
CVs	78%
Aptitude/ability tests	61%
Covering letters	58%
Personality questionnaires	43%
Assessment centres	30%
Telephone screening	18%
Biodata	4%
Graphology	1%

In its analysis of practices for the different occupational groups asked about, aptitude or ability tests were used by just over two-fifths of organisations for managerial and professional posts and for just over a quarter of skilled manual posts. Personality tests and assessment centres were more likely to be used for managerial and professional posts, but rarely for skilled manual. When asked for their views on the effectiveness of the various methods used, around three-quarters said that the selection interview was the most useful, but of those using assessment centres, a third or just above mentioned these as the most effective method. There was remarkably little support among respondents for ability or personality tests, with only a small percentage of respondents using these methods rating them the most effective, though there was some support for their use for manual worker selection.

As regards the assessment of effectiveness of the recruitment process, almost all respondents (97%) said that they did this. The most popular assessment method was informal feedback from line managers (81%), followed by analysing labour turnover (62%), subsequent appraisal ratings (57%) and results-based indicators (32%).

When compared with surveys of selection practices of ten or more years ago, the use of aptitude or ability tests, personality questionnaires and assessment centres have all shown significant growth in importance.

PART 2

Staff Retention

CHAPTER 4

Retention and labour turnover: a review of the issues

Having explored in the first three chapters techniques for recruiting and selecting candidates likely to be fitted for the role they are required to perform, we now turn our attention in the second part of the book to strategies for retaining them once we have got them.

The aim of this chapter is to provide a systematic framework for analysing retention and labour turnover issues. It first considers how labour turnover is measured and costed in order to provide a basis for comparing and benchmarking an organisation's performance in relation to others. Having measured and benchmarked labour turnover in order to establish whether a problem actually exists, the next step is to try and identify the causes of the problem and a number of factors said to influence an employee's decision to leave will be considered. Finally, the chapter considers what strategies have been offered to tackle problems of retention and labour turnover. Subsequent chapters explore these retention strategies in more detail.

Do we have a retention problem?

The problem of poor retention or its corollaries, 'wastage' or 'labour turnover', needs to be assessed within the context of the norms in a given external labour market. The propensity to leave an organisation can vary by age, length of service, industry sector, organisation size, occupational group and geographic location and it is important that a given level of turnover is not of itself seen as problematic. A level of turnover of 50% among retail sales staff in central London might be seen as acceptable, against a background in which 100% turnover was the external norm, but a 50% voluntary leaver rate among senior management of the same organisation would be likely to be a matter of considerable concern. Turnover needs measurement and benchmarking against realistic external comparators. Though there are a number of ways of measuring labour turnover, the most-used formula is:

$$\frac{\text{The number of leavers in a year}}{\text{Average number employed in a year}} \times 100$$

This is the formula most often used by organisations and is the one used by the regularly published surveys of labour turnover, for example by the CIPD (2000) and the CBI (2000a). In order to make external comparisons, the above formula should be calculated for each occupational group, since global labour turnover for an organisation as a whole is not very meaningful.

Factors influencing labour turnover

Turnover levels, having been calculated by occupational group, need to be assessed in the light of the range of factors which are said to influence turnover. The factors which influence turnover and the ways in which they do so are as follows:

- *Age*. It has generally been observed that labour turnover generally falls as age increases and thus a younger age profile within a given occupational group tends to push up turnover rates and vice versa.

- *Length of service*. It was identified many years ago (Rice et al., 1950) that the propensity to leave an organisation decreases with service and such a pattern normally shows up in statistical analyses of turnover by service. The research showed a characteristic 'survival' pattern for any given new cohort of employees. New entrants to an organisation experience three phases as they adjust to their new environment. First, some may experience an 'induction crisis' within the first few weeks or months as they discover that either the job or the organisation does not fit their expectations and leave. In the second phase, referred to as 'differential transit', employees go through a process of adjustment in which they further assess their job and the organisation and whether they see these as part of their longer-term future. Further turnover occurs during the 'differential transit' stage, but at lower levels than during the 'induction' crisis. Thereafter, those who survive the first two stages are said to form a 'settled connection' with the organisation and turnover diminishes further.

- *Industry sector.* Labour turnover tends to show characteristic variations by industry sector. The CIPD survey (2000), for example, found a range of turnover rates by sector ranging from 41% in hotels, restaurants and leisure at one end to just over 4% in the utilities at the other, with a national average across all sectors of just over 18%. Other sectors experiencing significantly higher than average levels of turnover included retailing (33%), construction (27%) and the IT industry (24%). Sectors experiencing turnover rates close to the national average (15 to 20%) included manufacturing, finance, local and central government and health, while education (13%), transport (13%) and the utilities (4%) experienced the lowest rates.

- *Organisation size.* It has generally been found that labour turnover decreases with organisation size. The CIPD (2000), for example, found turnover rates of just over 30% in organisations of less than 100 employees, falling steadily to close to 13% in organisations of 5,000 employees or more. The reasons for this may only be surmised, but may relate to the opportunities for career development and promotion and more generous reward packages available in larger organisations.

- *Occupational group.* The general principle is that the more senior the role in an organisation, the lower the rate of labour turnover. Thus, for example, the CIPD (2000) found turnover rates of management and professional staff in manufacturing of around 11%, skilled manual staff of close to 14%, clerical staff close to 19%, manual operatives at nearly 22% and unskilled manual staff at nearly 25%. These differences may reflect differing opportunities for career development within internal labour markets. The data also show that influences of the external labour market, recruitment difficulties and skills shortages can distort this general picture. For example, turnover among technical and scientific staff in manufacturing was relatively high at nearly 25%, while the problem in retailing and the hospitality sector was the retention of professional staff whose turnover rate was close to 23%.

- *Geographic location*. Local and regional labour market conditions also act to influence labour turnover rates. The CBI (1998) for example, found above average turnover rates in Scotland, the south-west and the south-east, below average rates in Wales, the south and the north-east and close to national average rates in the other regions. At one end, Scotland had a turnover rate of nearly 28%, while at the other, Yorkshire and Humberside had a rate of 6.5%.

The implications and costs of labour turnover

Labour turnover has significant costs and other less measurable disadvantages for organisations, but before considering these it is worth pausing to consider whether it might have any advantages. Potential advantages noted by Morris and Hodgins (2000) include:

- opportunities for promoting staff whose advancement might otherwise be blocked;

- opportunities to bring in new recruits with new ideas more in keeping with newly espoused cultures or values;

- opportunities to restructure or rationalise current methods of working;

- opportunities to change current methods of resourcing from in-house permanent staff to subcontracting, part-time working or other more flexible alternatives;

- opportunities to cut staffing costs through non-replacement and work reorganisation.

Thus labour turnover can be seen positively as an opportunity to bring about changes through natural wastage which otherwise might not have been available.

On the other hand, however, such opportunities need to be weighed against the considerable potential costs of losing staff with key skills and experience whom the organisation would have wished to retain and obviate the costs associated with their replacement. These costs include the following (Bevan, 1991; Fair, 1992; Taylor, 1998; Morris and Hodgins, 2000):

- administrative costs of processing leavers (e.g. payroll, pension, time taken by exit interviews, etc.);

- temporary replacement costs (e.g. use of temporary or agency staff, the use of overtime, disruptions to operations, and pressures placed on current staff while providing cover and their impact on morale and productivity);

- costs associated with the loss of knowledge, skills and experience of leavers;

- direct costs of recruiting replacements (e.g. advertising or agency fees);

- the time of staff administering the recruitment process;

- the time taken by staff in sifting, shortlisting and interviewing candidates – all the more so where psychometric tests or assessment centres are used – in addition to the costs of candidate expenses;

- the administrative costs associated with new starters, including payroll;

- the costs of inducting and training new staff;

- the salary costs of new staff during the learning period when they may be less productive.

According to the CIPD (2000), the average cost per leaver across all sectors, taking into account the administrative costs of processing leavers, the costs of recruiting replacements, training and unproductive time and indirect costs such as reduced customer service or satisfaction, was around £3,500 per annum. The highest replacement cost was found among professional staff at around £5,200 per leaver, management staff at £4,762 per leaver and technical or scientific staff at almost £4,000. It may be calculated that for an organisation with 1,000 employees experiencing the average rate of turnover of 18%, the annual cost would be close to £640,000, with a potential saving to be made of over £35,000 for each 1% reduction in turnover levels.

Some studies have calculated the costs of turnover in terms of an employee's equivalent annual salary. Morris and Hogdins (2000) report that this cost can vary from a half to one and a half times annual salary according to seniority, with the latter costs being experienced for more senior and highly paid staff. Fair (1992) suggests a broader range from the equivalent of six months' salary to as much as two years' salary for very senior posts while IDS (1995) puts the cost of turnover generally at around one and a half times salary. Another study of labour turnover costs at Quest Diagnostics, America's largest clinical testing firm, used a sophisticated costing model to calculate that at a turnover rate of 23% per annum, each leaver cost the firm the equivalent of three-quarters of their annual salary (Cooper, 2000b). The firm also calculated that a reduction of 5% in annual labour turnover would save $31 million (£22.7 million) a year. On closer investigation, they identified that a high number of people were leaving in their first year. By focusing on the selection process and presenting the job vacancy more clearly, together with measures to improve promotion prospects, labour turnover was halved over a two-year period with very significant cost savings. We may conclude, therefore, that while estimates of costs vary, all estimates point to labour turnover as being very costly for organisations.

As a guide to costing labour turnover, Fair (1992: 50) offers the pro forma shown in Figure 4.1 for costing wastage and calculating potential cost savings from any reductions achieved.

Sample Form for Calculation

Costing wastage and replacement

Enter number of employees	_____	(a),
Enter average weekly wage	£ _____	(b),
Multiply (a) × (b)	£ _____	(c),
Multiply (c) × 52	£ _____	(d) = *Total paybill*
Enter current wastage rate	_____ %	(e),
Enter average recruitment fees	_____ %	(f),
Multiply (d) × (e) × (f)	£ _____	(g),
Enter annual personnel staff costs	£ _____	(h),
Enter % time spent on recruitment	_____ %	(i),
Multiply (h) × (i) and add (g)	£ _____	(j) = *Administrative costs*
Enter average vacancy duration (days)	_____	(k),
Multiplier rate for overtime/temps.	_____	(l),
Multiply (b) × (l)	£ _____	(m),
Multiply (a) × (e) × (k) × [(m)/5]	£ _____	(n) = Unfilled vacancy costs
Enter skills training per starter (days)	_____	(o),
Enter daily cost of skills training	£ _____	(p),
Multiply (a) × (e) × (o) × (p)	£ _____	(q),
Enter learning curve duration (days)	_____	(r),
Enter non-productive % of learning curve	_____ %	(s),
Multiply (c) × (e) × [(r)/5] x (s)	£ _____	(t),
Add (q) + (t)	£ _____	(u) = Non-productive costs
Multiply (k) × [(c)/5] × (e)	£ _____	(v) = *Salary savings*
Add (n) + (u) − (v)	£ _____	(w) = *Replacement cost p.a.*

Potential cost saving

Enter reduced wastage rate	_____ %	(aa),
Subtract [(g) × (aa)]/(e) from (g)	£ _____	(bb),
Subtract [(w) × (aa)]/(e) from (w)	£ _____	(cc),
Enter current average LOS (months)	_____	(dd),
Enter new target average LOS (months)	_____	(ee),
Multiply [(ee)/(dd) − 1] × [(g) + (w)]	£ _____	(ff),
Expected vacancy reduction (days)	_____	(gg),
Multiply [(n) − (v)] × [(gg)/(k)]	£ _____	(hh),
Expected training reduction (days)	_____	(ii),
Multiply (q) × [(ii)/(o)]	£ _____	(jj),
Expected learning curve reduction (days)	_____	(kk),
Multiply (t) x [(kk)/(r)]	£ _____	(ll),
Add (bb) + (cc) + (ff) + (hh) + (jj) + (ll)	£ _____	(mm) = *Total savings p.a.*

Figure 4.1 Costing labour turnover. (*Source*: Fair, 1992: 50.)

The causes of turnover

Taylor (1998) quotes American research which identified the following ten-stage model underlying the 'employee turnover decision process':

1. Evaluate existing job.

2. Experience job satisfaction.

3. Think of quitting.

4. Evaluate expected utility of search for a new job and the costs of quitting.

5. Decide to search for alternatives.

6. Search for alternatives.

7. Evaluate alternatives.

8. Compare best alternative with present job.

9. Decide to quit.

10. Quit.

The key issue is what causes dissatisfaction and this can involve a host of possible reasons which will be considered below. Closely associated with this is the availability of alternatives. In times of economic downturn and higher unemployment, fewer opportunities present themselves and consequently labour turnover falls, with the opposite being the case in times of economic boom. Another constraint on finding alternatives in current conditions is an employee's age. Older age groups experience higher unemployment and have fewer job opportunities available to them compared with younger workers and it is therefore not surprising that labour turnover is lower among older rather than younger workers.

A number of specific causes of dissatisfaction at the workplace which potentially lead to a decision to leave have been identified and these have been outlined by Bevan (1991) as follows:

- the job, the organisation or its culture or values not meeting expectations;

- inadequate induction or further training;

- lack of intrinsic job satisfaction or motivation;

- lack of career development or perceived unfairness of promotion decisions;

- management style;

- flexible working arrangements;

- pay and benefits.

Each of these will be explored in more detail in the sections below.

The job, the organisation or its culture or values not meeting expectations

An apparently significant cause of leaving is that the job or the style of the organisation, as described at the time of recruitment, do not subsequently live up to expectations and have been 'oversold' or 'missold'. The result is likely to be an early decision to leave, described above as the 'induction crisis'. Underlying causes of this may include a lack of clarity about the selection criteria and the person sought to fill the post, the use of inadequate selection techniques or a lack of willingness to give realistic job information to candidates (see below). A further possible explanation is that employers, faced with skills shortage problems, feel under pressure to take a short-term view and fill a post without adequately considering whether a candidate is properly fitted. As Bevan (1991: 13) notes, by doing this, employers are effectively 'recruiting turnover'.

Inadequate standards of recruitment and selection can, therefore, be a significant cause of turnover and, as highlighted by Bevan (1991), an important consideration relates to the provision of realistic information to candidates about the job, the organisation and the prospects for career development and promotion, bearing in mind that candidates too are making a selection decision about their future. As Morris and Hodgins (2000: 14) have observed, 'organisations need to balance selling the job and presenting a true and honest picture during the recruitment and selection process'. Such an approach is known as the 'realistic job preview (RJP)'. Ivancevich (1995) reports the results of 15 RJP experiments in the United States involving over 5,000 people which revealed that RJPs resulted in an average 9% reduction in labour turnover, with greater effects among jobs involving high complexity, but lesser effects where jobs were low in complexity.

Ivancevich contrasts the 'traditional' job preview with the 'realistic' job preview. In the traditional approach, the following are the typical characteristics:

- Candidate expectations about the job are set too high.

- Jobs tend to be presented as attractive, stimulating and challenging.

- The presentation of the job in this way yields a high rate of acceptances in relation to offers.

- Subsequent experience in the job causes disillusionment when expectations are unfulfilled.

- Dissatisfaction results from the gap between expectations and reality.

- The gap between expectations and reality increase the probability that an individual will leave.

By contrast, the realistic job preview, according to Ivancevich (1995) is characterised as follows:

- Job expectations are set at realistic levels, balancing advantages and disadvantages.

- The provision of realistic information better enables candidates to assess whether the job meets their needs.

- Acceptance rates after offer fall because realistic information will have discouraged some applicants.

- Job experience reaffirms the expectations set out.

- Satisfaction levels are higher as expectations are met.

- The better fit between expectations and reality reduce the probability that an individual will leave.

Realistic job previews, Ivancevich (1995) concludes, recognise that jobs and their organisational contexts have more attractive and less attractive features and while providing an open and honest picture of these reduces acceptance rates, those who accept a post 'warts and all' are more likely to be satisfied with their decision and more likely to stay.

Inadequate induction and further training

A lack of appropriate induction and early job training can be further causes of the 'induction crisis'. New employees who experience any of the following are likely to suffer early disillusionment which may lead to a decision to leave:

- where they are given little understanding of what the work of their organisation is and how their activities fit in;

- where they are not given clear instructions about their duties;

- where they are given little attention by their supervisor or manager and made to feel welcome;

- where they are set demanding targets from their first day.

Strategies for tackling this cause of turnover are considered further in Chapter 5.

Lack of intrinsic job satisfaction and motivation

Research has not identified a close causal relationship generally between lack of job satisfaction and the propensity to leave, mainly because variables other than satisfaction intervene (Robbins, 1993). As noted earlier, the decision to leave is bounded by constraints concerning the alternative options available and thus an employee who sees few alternatives to their current job is likely to remain even though the job itself is a source of little satisfaction. On the other hand, closer relationships have been found between employee motivation, their willingness to exert effort in pursuit of organisational goals in order to satisfy personal needs, and a decision to leave. For employees with personal growth needs, who probably represent the majority, links have been established between the content and variety of their jobs and the decision to stay or go. Where variety and scope to develop intrinsic job interest are lacking, employees are more likely to leave (Robbins, 1993). Thus, the design of jobs assumes some significance when measures to improve retention are under consideration and this will be considered further in Chapter 6.

Lack of career development or perceived unfairness of promotion decisions

Two issues interrelate here according to Bevan (1991). First, employees may leave because the organisation is unable to offer much in the way of career development and promotion opportunities and the only option available for an employee seeking advancement may be to move elsewhere. The reasons for this may be manyfold: career blockages caused by lack of turnover; moves to flatter, delayered organisation structures; industries experiencing slow growth or even decline. There are, nevertheless, measures which organisations might consider, even when faced with these objective situations and we shall return to these in Chapter 7.

A second issue relates to some perceived unfairness on the part of the employee about how promotion decisions are taken in situations where promotion opportunities are available. Perceptions of equity and fair treatment are important influences on employee motivation. According to Adams' equity theory (1965), we expect a fair balance between our 'inputs' to a job, in terms of skills, knowledge and effort expended, and the 'outcomes' from the job. Expected outcomes will vary from person to person and may include fair pay in relation to others, intrinsically satisfying work and fair opportunities to be considered for promotion in line with our perceptions of the efforts expended. Where we perceive some imbalance in the 'inputs/outcomes' equation, the result will be demotivation unless we are able to rationalise the apparent inequity some other way, and a decision to leave becomes more likely. As will be discussed in Chapter 7, systems of performance management and performance appraisal on which many decisions about promotion are based are fraught with problems of objectivity, and perceptions about how related decisions about performance-related pay are taken can serve to compound the problem of perceived inequity.

Management style

The style of managers and supervisors can have a strong influence on decisions about staying or going. Bevan (1991) quotes research among a group of leavers who were asked about the quality of management and supervision which they had expected and that which they had experienced in the company which had influenced their decision to leave. The leavers said that they had expected from management or supervision:

- constructive feedback;

- respect and the encouragement of loyalty;

- fair assessment of performance;

- interesting and challenging work;

- personal support.

What they actually got was as follows:

- unapproachability;

- a distant and uncaring attitude;

- inconsistent assessment and favouritism;

- lack of consultation.

Buckingham (2000) has suggested that employees leave their managers, not their organisations, and Bevan's conclusions on the basis of the above research findings were similar. Managers held the key to retaining staff and retention rates were better where managers more closely met employee expectations regarding treatment than where managers exhibited characteristics such as those in the latter checklist above.

Flexible working arrangements

Flexible working arrangements, now increasingly bound up with the emerging debate on the 'work–life balance', are increasingly being used in explicit recognition of the conflicting demands placed on employees when seeking to balance commitment to their job with commitments to other aspects important in their lives, such as family or leisure interests. The sharper focus on performance, both on the part of the organisation as a whole and the individuals within it, which emerged strongly during the 1990s, is now being recognised paradoxically as a source of constraints on performance improvement. A culture of long and unsocial hours and the increased incidence of stress at work have exacerbated the delicate work–life balance and solutions are being sought in such areas as 'diversity', 'family-friendly' policies and more flexible working arrangements. Recent evidence indicates that the introduction of such policies can offer facilities to help people manage potential conflicts in maintaining a more appropriate work–life balance and can also contribute to the retention of people who might otherwise have left. The role of work–life balance policies in a retention strategy will be considered further in Chapter 8.

Pay and benefits

Pay – and to a lesser extent benefits – is often seen by organisations as the main cause of their turnover problem. However, as Bevan (1991) points out, dissatisfaction with pay is less often concerned with the absolute amount paid and more often about the perceived fairness of pay in relation to others (within the organisation or outside it) and the way that pay is administered within the organisation. He notes that studies of satisfaction levels with pay in most cases show no difference between stayers and leavers: both groups show equal levels of dissatisfaction! An offer of more pay, he concludes, will help to keep about 10% of people who might otherwise have left, but dissatisfaction with other aspects of the job is the more common cause of resignation. In a similar vein, Hiltrop (1999) notes in relation to reasons for leaving among managers that the level of pay is not highly significant, provided that it is not well out of line with the market, and more important were pride in the company and trust in their chief executive's ability to take decisions. The same sort of conclusions were reached by Pricewaterhouse-Coopers (2000) who identified in their survey benchmarking HR practice a belief among employers that money alone is not enough to induce staff to stay: a good remuneration package needs to be accompanied by opportunities for staff development and an enriching working environment.

Though firms need to be competitive in relation to pay levels in the market, it needs to be borne in mind that labour markets operate in ways far from the purist notions of the classical economist. Research has shown that even in a local labour market, people have limited information about the pay rates on offer and differences of as much as 50% have been found for the same type of work (Claydon, 1997). Moreover, people's ability to move jobs may be constrained by family or other commitments restricting their mobility and economists also refer to 'inertia' or 'sentiment' to explain why other attachments, such as congenial colleagues, job satisfaction, job security or a host of factors other than rates of pay, keep people from moving jobs. Moreover, many organisations have created 'internal labour markets', closely bound up with programmes of training, development and internal promotion hierarchies, which provide avenues for employees to progress within, rather than seek opportunities outside an organisation. Though pay cannot be ruled out as a cause of retention problems, particularly where there are severe skills shortages, other factors considered in this section have been shown to be of greater importance when seeking to tackle these problems. The issue of reward management and retention will be revisited in Chapter 7.

Pinpointing the causes of labour turnover in our own organisation

While many possible causes of labour turnover have been considered, it is important that the specific causes are identified in our own organisation. Thus an obvious starting point is our own data and it is important that the rate of turnover, using the formula given on p. 102, is calculated for each department, occupational group or grade and location. This will help to pinpoint where particular problems are being experienced, though it is important that our rates of turnover in any of these categories are compared with external benchmark data, as described earlier, in order to identify whether our experience is markedly different from other organisations. We may, however, take the view that although our level of turnover reflects external norms, we wish to do better and bring turnover rates down below these norms. It may, in addition, be useful to analyse turnover by various length of service categories in order to identify whether the nature of our turnover problem relates to short-term stayers or longer-serving employees. The former might point to problems of recruitment, selection and induction, while the latter might point to problems of career development and promotion opportunities.

Data on labour turnover is useful for identifying where a problem lies, but does not provide specific information about its causes for which qualitative data, rather than quantitative data, is required. A useful source of such data is from exit interviews and if these are not used, they are worth introducing. These involve asking the employee why they are leaving in order to gather more qualitative data about the underlying causes of turnover. As Taylor (1998) points out, however, one problem associated with an exit interview is obtaining the real reasons for leaving. The departing employee may be reliant on obtaining a good reference and may be reluctant to stir up any controversy, especially if the reason relates to their manager who may be asked to write a reference. Taylor therefore suggests that an exit interview is better conducted by someone impartial, such as a personnel officer. In order for exit interviews to be conducted on a standardised basis, it may also be useful to devise a questionnaire for completion by the departing employee soon after their notice has been received and to discuss what the employee has put at the exit interview. The questionnaire can be designed so as to include all the possible causes discussed above and organisations may wish to add other possible causes in the light of their specific circumstances. Against each possible cause, the questionnaire could also usefully invite the leaver to assess the strength of each possible cause by stating whether the cause was 'very important', 'quite important', 'of little importance' or 'not important'. Cumulative data gathered from exit interviews might help to show some common pattern and point to some issues which need addressing, if practicable. Going beyond exit interviews, it is also possible to mount some more extensive research into reasons for leaving, especially where exit interview data is unavailable, by mailing questionnaires to those who have left. The content of such a questionnaire would be similar to the exit questionnaire described above.

Which strategies have proved effective in enhancing retention?

Various surveys have asked employers what strategies they employ to enhance retention and reduce turnover and to provide an assessment of their effectiveness. The results of these surveys therefore provide guidance on the approaches felt to be helpful.

IDS (2000) identified that the following measures were reported as effective by employers responding to their retention survey:

- better recruitment and selection;

- improved induction arrangements;

- more focus on staff development and the provision of more intrinsically interesting work;

- the introduction of flexible, family-friendly policies;

- the provision of attractive employee benefits.

By way of case examples, they quoted an example from a Japanese-owned manufacturing company in Telford which brought very high turnover rates of nearly 100% per annum down to nearly a third of this over a two-year period by extending induction from a half-day programme to four weeks, involving a mix of off-the-job training and work on a production line under close supervision. Recruitment was also reviewed, with a greater emphasis on targeting employees who could demonstrate stability. As well as reference checks, they also reconsidered their previous policy of employing younger workers and targeted the full age range. Aptitude testing was also introduced to improve assessment of suitability for production work. At Glaxo, measures were put in place to encourage women returners and improve retention rates after maternity leave, including childcare allowances, return-to-work bonuses and the encouragement of part-time working and jobsharing among returnees. These measures resulted in improvements in return rates from around 55% to 90%. Asda's retention strategies were linked to the provision of an employee share ownership scheme, requiring employees to remain for some years in order to achieve gains, together with more emphasis on internal promotion from the shop floor. These strategies have helped Asda to achieve levels of labour turnover of around 25% per annum, compared with closer to 100% experienced by some employers in the retailing sector.

In a survey of staff turnover by Reed (1998), companies were asked to say which measures were proving effective in bringing down labour turnover and their replies, in rank order, were as follows:

1. Improved training of staff (70%)

2. Better career development and career progression opportunities (58%)

3. Increased staff recognition (41%)

4. Multi-skilling (40%)

5. Measures to improve team-building (39%)

6. Development of cross-divisional career opportunities (29%)

7. Increased salaries above the rate of inflation (27%)

8. Improvements to the physical working environment (24%)

9. Performance-related pay (24%).

A survey by IRS (1999a) also asked employers about which policies were effective in bringing down turnover and their replies, in rank order, were as follows:

1. Training initiatives (70%)

2. Improved recruitment and selection (64%)

3. Providing employees with opportunities to gain qualifications (55%)

4. Improved induction processes (52%)

5. Improved career development planning (44%)

6. Multi-skilling (30%)

7. Opportunities to develop skills more broadly beyond current role (27%)

8. Better succession planning (20%)

9. Use of mentoring schemes (17%)

10. Policies of clawing back education and training costs from leavers (10%).

In terms of initiatives relating to culture and style, half of respondents said that improved organisational communications had helped retention, almost 40% said that flexible working hours had done so and a third said that policies of empowering staff had contributed. As regards improving retention through pay, a third said that increases in basic pay had proved effective, though few supported the use of retention bonuses.

Staff retention was identified by PricewaterhouseCoopers' (2000) *HR Benchmarking Report 2000* as the key HR issue by 80% of their respondent organisations and the strategies most frequently used to retain staff, in order of importance, were as follows:

1. Providing development opportunities (81%)

2. Changing organisational culture and values (57%)

3. Improving working conditions (52%)

4. Having clear job definitions and objectives (48%)

5. Providing more bonus opportunities (38%)

6. Increasing base salaries (33%)

7. Increasing fringe benefits (24%)

8. Job enrichment programmes (19%).

While not commenting specifically on the effectiveness of the strategies implemented by the organisations replying to the survey, it highlighted the overriding importance of career development as a strategy for staff retention and concluded that this was far more important than the attractiveness of the reward package.

One final piece of research may be quoted with regard to the question of effective strategies for retention. Hiltrop (1999) sought to establish whether there were any links between human resource management practices and the ability of companies to attract and retain management staff. Having obtained independent assessments of companies' abilities to attract and retain management staff, the companies were asked to say which of over 60 human resource management practices applied in their organisations. The practices operating in organisations rated as 'superior' in terms of recruiting and retaining staff, in rank order from the most important, were as follows:

1. Opportunities for teamworking and participation

2. Opportunities for training and skill development

3. Proactive human resource planning and strategic human resource management

4. Giving staff autonomy to make decisions within a framework of decentralised decision-making

5. Extra rewards and recognition for high performance

6. Opportunities for career development and provision of career guidance

7.   Openness of information about corporate goals and plans.

What may be concluded about any common themes emerging from all these surveys investigating retention of staff? A common feature of all of them is the prime importance of education and training, including induction, opportunities for developing skills through performing interesting and varied roles in the context of teams and opportunities for career development. Thereafter, effective recruitment and selection emerge as the second priority in any retention strategy. As a third priority, opportunities for greater flexibility of working hours and arrangements appear to offer scope for enhancing retention. Fourthly, though responses varied, the role of reward and recognition of high performance emerged as being of some importance in retention strategies.

In the light of the apparent importance of these issues in enhancing retention, it is to these that we turn specifically in the remaining chapters, with the exception of recruitment and selection which was considered in Part 1.

CHAPTER 5

The role of induction in staff retention

We noted in Chapter 4 that employees are most at risk of leaving during the first few weeks and months of their new employment and that a number will experience an 'induction crisis' as they come to grips with the job they have taken and whether it really meets the expectations which they had on accepting it. It was also noted in Chapter 4 that improving induction arrangements was seen as an important element in a retention strategy according to the views expressed by employers in response to a survey by IDS (2000). Starting a new job has also been recognised as a stressful process, with much that is unfamiliar and much to be learned (Wanous, 1992, in Taylor, 1998). It follows from this that the process of inducting employees into the organisation and the management of their progress in the early months have significant roles to play in a retention strategy. A useful example of how this should not be managed is provided by Bevan (1991) who quotes an example from an insurance company and the experience of new clerical staff in their first few days. As well as increasing the number of claims to be processed on each of their first three days, accuracy levels were monitored, with 90% accuracy expected on the first day, 95% on the second and 100% from the third day on. Turnover rates among these staff exceeded 60%. Not surprisingly, Bevan emphasises the importance of setting realistic targets and standards for achievement during the early period of employment, the provision of feedback on progress and the need to ensure that learning rather than just exposure to the job is taking place.

Induction as 'socialisation'

Induction is essentially a process of socialising new employees into the organisation in order that they may quickly feel an integral part of their work team and become a valued member of it. The stronger the culture of the organisation and the more specific the characteristic ways of doing things, the more important it is for induction to inculcate cultural values. It is not surprising to find that organisations with particularly strong and characteristic cultures invest considerable time and resources in induction.

Robbins (1993) sees socialisation as a three-stage process: pre-arrival, encounter and metamorphosis. The 'pre-arrival' stage of socialisation recognises that certain expectations will have been established before arriving in the organisation. Though some of these will be preconceptions, what has been said and the impressions gained during the recruitment and selection process will also have played an important role in setting expectations. Thus the recruitment and selection of all staff, including those not subsequently selected, needs to be seen as part of the socialisation process. As noted in Chapter 4, the giving of open and frank information about the job and the organisation through 'realistic job previews', rather than painting an unrealistically rosy picture, is an important part of socialisation prior to arrival and can do much to help a candidate weigh their decision to join or not and also shape attitudes and expectations about the job they are accepting. During the second stage of socialisation, the 'encounter' stage, the new employee compares the realities with what they have been led to expect and any disillusionment will increase the probability of their leaving, thus further confirming the importance of a realistic job preview in any retention strategy. By the third stage, 'metamorphosis', the employee has undergone a process of adaptation and change and become a settled and integrated member of the organisation's staff. Any gaps between expectations and reality have been both reconcilable and reconciled and the employee has learned not only the formal requirements of their role, but also the informal practices and ways of doing things.

Robbins concludes that the achievement of 'metamorphosis' requires particular approaches to induction. First, socialisation should be formal rather than informal. Under formal socialisation, new employees are separated to some extent from the normal work routine and undergo a planned programme of learning, while under informal socialisation, the employee is put directly into their job with minimal instruction and little or no special attention. Second, the programme of learning should be of fixed rather than indeterminate length. Fixed-length programmes should specify in a realistic way what needs to have been learned and in what timescale, with feedback on progress, and set measurable targets to achieve in order to help the employee pass from entry mode to becoming a fully accepted and integrated member of the organisation. Programmes of indeterminate length mean that these targets are unclear and the transition into fully accepted and integrated member less clear-cut and understood. Third, effective socialisation programmes should include the use of role modelling. New employees should be assigned at an early stage to role models, also referred to as mentors or 'buddies', in order to understand both the formal and also the informal ways in which things are done, rather than being left to their own devices.

Induction as a 'process' rather than an 'event'

A traditional view of induction saw it as a course or programme varying in length from an hour or two on the first morning to something more extensive and lasting for the first week or more. By contrast, Robbins' (1993) model of socialisation, noted above, emphasises the importance of seeing induction as a planned and ongoing process with a finite time limit beginning before an employee starts work and continuing for a period of months. This reflects the reality that people cannot take in all that they need to know through densely packed initial instruction and that formal programmes of information-giving are inappropriate for imparting understanding of the more informal aspects and ways of working.

A planned approach to induction recognises, as noted earlier, that it begins with what has been said during the process of recruitment and selection. It also needs to recognise that the induction process is likely to contain both standardised and personally tailored elements. Induction needs not only to include standard information which each new employee needs to know about the organisation, but also incorporate an individual training plan (or personal development plan) drawn up from an early stage establishing some personal learning targets tailored to individual learning needs. With the growth of competency frameworks for recruitment and selection, information will have been gathered through competency-based selection techniques about an individual's personal competencies in relation to those required by the job. From this, it may have been identified that while the new recruit provided a good match with most of the competencies required by their role, there were some critical priority areas for development in order for them to perform effectively. For example, where an employee has been recruited into a managerial role for the first time, they might have had no previous experience of budgetary control. If an understanding of this is a central requirement, then opportunities to learn about this ought to be built into an individually tailored induction programme for this employee. Thus, effective induction programmes consist of both standard elements and personally tailored elements, and many organisations document these in an induction training plan which contains both standard and individually tailored elements agreed between the new employee and their manager. Such plans also contain provisions for assessing competencies and a sign-off procedure to record that this has happened (Reid and Barrington, 1994).

Roberts (1997) suggests that the process of induction, having commenced at the recruitment stage, can usefully continue immediately after acceptance without waiting until the first morning when the employee arrives. For example, further written information can be given about the organisation as a whole, its recent history and its mission, culture, vision and values where these are explicitly stated. For more senior posts, information might also be given about the current work of the department which the employee will be joining and possibly also some of the activities which they will be involved in from an early stage. He goes on to suggest that in the early period of employment, a balance should be struck between purely learning activities and the performance of real tasks.

The first day should be concerned with familiarising the employee with the geography of the workplace, providing opportunities to meet and get to know the people with whom they will be working and getting familiar with health, safety and hygiene issues. The remainder of the first week should be mainly job-focused and by the end of the first week the new employee should have become familiar with the purpose of their own role, the objectives of their team or department and know their key internal and external contacts. Familiarisation with more general administrative and organisational matters can, in Roberts' view, wait until after the first week and can be communicated at a number of half-day sessions attended at periodic intervals while continuing on-the-job learning or other planned competency development. Roberts suggests that the learning content of induction sessions designed to cover more general administrative matters can usefully be packaged into modules run at regular intervals. In this way, it may be possible for new starters entering at various different times to attend each of these in any order and so maximise the number of recent entrants attending any given session.

Following Robbins' emphasis on the importance of role-modelling, a number of writers (Skeats, 1991; Harrison, 1992; Roberts, 1997; Taylor, 1998) recommend that each new employee should be assigned to mentors or 'buddies'. Taylor (1998) notes that this person should be approximately the same age as and have a similar status to the new starter, with a good knowledge of their job. The mentor or buddy can usefully be introduced to the new employee before their start date and take responsibility from the first day for showing them around and introducing them to key people, and play an ongoing supportive role during the induction period and beyond.

The content of formal induction programmes

Induction programmes contain a mix of standard information, job and department-specific information and tailored personal development. This final section is concerned with what it is recommended should be communicated by way of standardised information about the organisation and its administrative arrangements.

Marchington and Wilkinson (2000) suggest that three perspectives can be identified in relation to the functions performed by induction. The best known and probably most widely practised is termed its 'administrative' function. This perspective is most closely associated with the standardised induction programme, designed to impart information about the administrative arrangements of the organisation and is the main concern of this section. They also identify what they term the 'welfare' and 'human resource management' functions of induction. While the welfare aspects, helping the new employee to settle in, lie mainly in the hands of their manager, a buddy or mentor (if used) and other close departmental colleagues, the 'human resource management' functions of induction can feature in both departmental induction and in more standardised, formal induction sessions.

This latter perspective on induction is tied up with socialisation and the role of induction in educating new employees and inculcating the organisation's ethos, culture and values. Where strong cultures exist, organisations will be concerned to transmit these to new employees. Indeed, the new employee's first contact with the organisation, the style of the job advertisement, the company logo on the letterhead and application form, the content of the application form, accompanying correspondence and company literature, the appearance of the building internally and externally visited by the employee for interview, the content and style of the interview or other assessment techniques and the behaviour of the interviewers themselves, will all have served to communicate messages about organisational culture. In strong cultures, the messages conveyed will have been carefully managed, while in weaker cultures they will have been left to the random interpretation of the applicant.

Culture is transmitted through artefacts and symbols, language, myths and stories and rituals (Robbins, 1993). Symbols and language will already have served to communicate cultural messages during the selection process and stories which typify what the culture is about may have already been told. Induction in strong cultures will, from the very start, be concerned to reinforce and transmit organisational culture to the new starters.

As Marchington and Wilkinson (2000) note, such artefacts and symbols as dress codes or the wearing of company uniforms will soon become evident after joining an organisation. The use of phrases such as 'associates', 'the team' or the 'family' to denote employees will convey cultural messages. Early in the induction process, either within the department or in a formal induction session, new employees will begin to hear the myths and stories of the heroic deeds of legendary employees and more formally new employees will be given a clear message about the mission, culture and values of the organisation and the pattern of behaviour expected. If, for example, customer service, teamworking, quality or empowerment lie at the heart of company values, strong messages will be communicated early in induction about the expected behaviours associated with these values. Harrison (1992) refers to this as 'dialogic learning', the process of understanding the culture of the organisation and integrating the goals, values, attitudes and patterns of behaviour of the individual with those of the organisation.

Moving on to the 'administrative' functions of induction, the most important aspect for many organisations, there is general agreement that new employees should be given information about the following at formal induction sessions (Croner.CCH, 2000; Reid and Barrington, 1994; Marchington and Wilkinson, 2000):

- the organisation, its mission, values, vision, history, products or services, organisation structure and its future growth plans;

- hours of work, shift arrangements, timekeeping and any time-recording arrangements;

- health, safety and security arrangements, including safety rules and procedures, hazards, provision and wearing of protective equipment, first aid and accident procedures, no smoking rules, wearing of ID badges, fire alarms, fire drills and assembly points, safety committees, safety representatives;

- pay, pay scales, method of payment, hours of work, times of breaks, overtime, holiday entitlement, holiday pay and associated arrangements, sick pay and absence reporting procedures, operation of any performance-related pay schemes, bonuses, profit-sharing or share option schemes, expense claims, benefits, pension arrangements and life assurance schemes;

- social and welfare, including canteen, toilets, first aid or medical facilities, sports and social facilities, rest rooms, provision of clothing, discount schemes, counselling or employee assistance programmes;

- company rules and procedures, including discipline and grievance procedures, equal opportunity policies, works rules, quality standards (e.g. ISO 9000), trade union agreements, trade union membership, staff associations;

- education, training and development, including support available for further or continuing education, content of internal training programmes, internal vacancies and promotion opportunities.

In conclusion, labour turnover statistics nearly always show that an employee is at high risk of leaving during the early stage of their employment, the so called 'induction crisis', and there is much evidence, including survey evidence based on employers' experiences (IDS, 2000), to indicate that well planned and implemented induction arrangements form an important part of any effective strategy for staff retention.

CHAPTER 6

Designing jobs which motivate and retain staff

We saw in Chapter 4 that close relationships had been found between motivation and satisfaction of people's needs through the content and variety in their jobs and their decision to stay or leave (Robbins, 1993; Bevan, 1991) and it was concluded that the design of jobs so as to provide intrinsic satisfaction assumed some importance when considering strategies for retention. The importance of job design also emerged from the results of surveys of employers' retention strategies. IDS (2000) identified that greater focus on employee development and the provision of more intrinsically interesting work featured prominently in employers' responses. Such related issues as skill development, multiskilling and opportunities for teamworking also featured prominently in

---

other surveys of employers' retention strategies (Reed, 1998; IDS, 1999; Hiltrop, 1999; PricewaterhouseCoopers, 2000). The aim of this chapter is, therefore, to explore what is meant by employee motivation and draw conclusions about how jobs may be designed or redesigned so as to enhance motivation and retention.

What is motivation?

Motivation in the work context is concerned with the factors which drive employees towards the achievement of desired organisational goals. Two early theories which implicitly attempted to explain motivation came from F.W. Taylor (1911) and Elton Mayo (1933; Roethlisberger and Dickson, 1939). Taylor, writing after the turn of the century, strongly emphasised the importance of cash reward, seeing employees as primarily motivated by money, and was much concerned with devising incentive payments that motivated employees to produce high levels of output. The view that economic motivation is an important driver behind human behaviour has remained influential, as evidenced by the upsurge of interest in performance-related pay. Mayo, on the other hand, identified that a primary motivator at work stemmed from social needs, commitment to colleagues and the need for involvement in work-related decisions. Where opportunities to earn high incentive payments conflicted with employees' group interests, as reflected in peer pressures, social needs would override economic incentives. Interest in work groups has remained an enduring one since and, as we shall see later, there has been much renewed interest in organising work around teams in recent years.

During the last fifty years, considerable research has been undertaken by organisational psychologists into trying to understand motivation in the workplace and three broad schools of thought have emerged about what motivates people at work. The first of these schools of thought have been classified as 'content' or 'needs' theorists – 'needs' theorists because they have focused on the internalised needs which all people have and which, if satisfied at work, result in motivation and 'content' theorists because their proposals have focused on the elements in job content which motivate. These theories have produced universal prescriptions about what motivates people and have enjoyed popularity because of their ready applicability at a workplace. Their ideas are also particularly relevant to job design because they have generated a considerable amount of information about the content of jobs in relation to motivation. The second group, 'process' theorists', see the process of motivation as more complex and varying from individual to individual and are concerned more with the processes of 'how' motivation is created rather than with 'what' motivates people universally. While less concerned with prescriptions about job content and motivation, they have nevertheless produced some important ideas which need to be taken on board when considering what needs to be done to enhance motivation. The third group, who have been labelled 'socio-technical systems' theorists, draw from both psychological and sociological perspectives and have used systems theory to explain work behaviour in terms of social attitudes both inside and outside a workplace and their interrelationships with the technology employed to perform work tasks. All three perspectives and their implications for job design will be considered below.

Motivation through job content

The origins of the idea that people could achieve motivation through the work that they perform can be traced to the ideas of Maslow (1943) and his notion of 'self-actualisation'. Maslow proposed a 'hierarchy of needs' to explain human motivation as follows:

- *Physiological needs.* These represent the basic needs for human survival, including food and shelter.

- *Safety needs.* These represent a need for a safe environment.

- *Social needs.* Needs for affection, friendship and belonging.

- *Esteem needs.* These include the need for both self-esteem, a feeling of self-worth, and the esteem of others which results in status and recognition.

- *Self-actualisation.* This represents the achievement of self-fulfilment and achieving all that an individual is capable of.

The needs are seen in terms of a hierarchy in which a lower need must be fulfilled before a person is driven to fulfil the next need in the hierarchy. In the context of work, the lower order needs (physiological and safety) may be seen as largely fulfilled outside employing organisations in industrialised societies, but the higher order needs may potentially be fulfilled by the work that people do. In terms of the design of jobs in Maslow's theory, work that provides social fulfilment, opportunities for status and recognition and, most importantly, self-actualisation or self-fulfilment will have the potential to motivate if these elements are built in.

Maslow's hierarchy was revisited some years later by Alderfer (1972) who came up with a modified version of it in his 'ERG Theory', standing for existence needs, relatedness needs and growth needs. Existence needs reflected Maslow's physiological and safety needs; relatedness reflected Maslow's social needs and the external component of esteem needs; and growth needs – the desire for personal development and achieving one's potential – incorporated Maslow's needs for self-esteem and self-actualisation. Like Maslow, he identified that satisfaction of a lower need drove people on to achieve a higher need, but in addition found that where a lower order need ceased to be met, people would regress and be motivated to fulfil the lower need. A practical application of this idea may be taken from a situation in which someone who has been enjoying career advancement and is highly motivated by their work is faced with the threat of redundancy. This threatens a lower order need, the need for security, and can impact negatively on motivation even though the job itself has not changed. Thus motivation through self-actualisation or 'growth needs' may be negatively affected by job insecurity and Alderfer's ideas remind us that a secure working environment may be a necessary precondition for motivating staff even where jobs have been designed to provide variety and intrinsic interest.

Some of the most influential ideas about designing jobs for motivational purposes have emanated from the work of Herzberg (1966, 1968). In many respects, Herzberg's ideas reflect an attempt to refine Maslow's theory about lower and higher order needs. By carrying out a series of interviews, initially with engineers and accountants and later with a wider range of occupational groups, he asked respondents to refer to a time when they felt exceptionally good or exceptionally bad about their job. When he classified the results, he identified that people referred to the following in relation to exceptionally good events at work and he termed these 'satisfiers' or 'motivators':

- achievement

- recognition

- the work itself

- responsibility

- personal growth and advancement.

The exceptionally bad events referred to, which he termed 'dissatisfiers' or 'hygiene factors', were as follows:

- company policy and administration

- relations with supervisor

- working conditions

- salary

- interpersonal relationships

- status

- security.

Herzberg concluded that the factors which caused satisfaction and dissatisfaction were different. Those which caused satisfaction and therefore motivation related to the intrinsic features of the job: the more these were present, the more someone would be motivated and conversely, the less they were present or totally lacking, the less they would be motivated. The dissatisfiers or 'hygiene' factors (i.e. factors relevant to the context of the job rather than the job itself) were a potential source of dissatisfaction. Thus, for example, the award of a higher salary or provision of more status might reduce a cause of dissatisfaction, but its effect would only be temporary and would not serve to motivate higher levels of achievement. As will be discussed below, Herzberg went on to advocate the concept of 'job enrichment' as a means of building the motivators which he identified into people's jobs. While Herzberg's research probably played down the role of monetary reward and the importance of individual differences, it did focus on the importance of the content of jobs as a source of motivation and this idea remains influential. Thus, in terms of building a framework for designing jobs for motivation and retention, the content of jobs needs to incorporate the factors listed above as 'motivators', while the work context needs to consider the elements listed as 'hygiene' factors since these can be a source of dissatisfaction.

A final set of ideas about the link between job content and motivation may be taken from Hackman et al.'s (1975) 'job characteristics model of work motivation', which proposes that the following five core job dimensions are sought by all employees:

1. *Skill variety* – the need for jobs to contain a variety of activities involving the use of different skills.

2. *Task identity* – the need for jobs to contain the completion of a whole and identifiable piece of work.

3. *Task significance* – the need for jobs to be seen, either within the organisation or outside it, as significant rather than trivial.

4. *Autonomy* – the need for jobs to provide some scope for making independent decisions.

5. *Feedback* – the importance of obtaining feedback based on the results of job performance.

In terms of the outcomes and impact on motivation, Hackman and Oldham concluded that points 1 to 3 above created a feeling of meaningfulness in the work which generated high motivation. Point 4, autonomy, created a feeling of responsibility for the outcomes of the work and generated job satisfaction and high performance. Point 5, feedback, enhanced commitment and quality of performance through knowledge of the results and opportunities to improve work effectiveness.

Process theories of motivation

Rather than focusing on human needs and what ought to be built into people's jobs in order to motivate, process theory views motivation as the result of a set of interconnected variables which influence behaviour and motivation. These include expectancy theory, equity theory and goal theory, each of which will be considered below.

Expectancy theory sees motivation in terms of people's perceived expectations and is associated with the ideas of Vroom (1964) and Porter and Lawler (1968). In broad terms, it proposes that people will be motivated by their perceptions of the link between desired outcomes and the effort that they are prepared to expend. However, the outcomes that people expect from their jobs can vary considerably from person to person: monetary reward, status, recognition, job security, opportunities to socialise and in some cases job satisfaction. Thus while job satisfaction may be important for some people, motivation is concerned with identifying desired outcomes and thus expectancy theory is a useful reminder that attention is required to both intrinsic job satisfaction and extrinsic rewards, such as the pay and conditions, if motivation is to occur.

Equity theory is associated with the work of J.S. Adams (1965) and has been found by research to be an important explanation of motivation. Moreover, its ideas underpin much of reward management practice. The theory suggests that perceptions of 'fairness', as reflected in the popular saying 'a fair day's work for a fair day's pay', is an important factor in human motivation. Adams' equity theory suggests that employees assess the effort–reward relationship by weighing all the inputs into a job (e.g. skills, effort, knowledge, experience, etc.) in relation to all the outcomes received by way of reward (e.g. pay, job satisfaction, security, status, etc.). Where we feel that there is a fair balance between the total inputs to a job and total outcomes from it, equity exists and we feel motivated. These assessments are subjective on the part of the individual and are arrived at by comparing ourselves with others around us, either within an organisation or with others outside the employing organisation. Demotivation can occur when we perceive that inequity exists. According to Adams, employees may respond in a number of ways on discovery of inequity, as follows:

- *Change inputs.* Since equity depends on perceptions of a fair balance between inputs and reward outcomes, which may either relate to intrinsic job satisfaction or extrinsic cash reward, perceptions of balance may be restored, for example, by reducing inputs (e.g. reduced effort) where the outcomes are seen as inadequate or increasing inputs (e.g. increased effort) where outcomes are seen as generous in comparison with others.

- *Change outcomes.* Another way of restoring balance between perceived inputs and outcomes is to try and influence the outcomes side of the equation. Thus if pay is perceived as inadequate in relation to the inputs, a pay increase may be sought; if the problem relates to intrinsic job satisfaction, attempts may be made to redress these problems with one's manager in order to achieve desired changes in job content.

- *Change the basis of comparison.* Another way of rationalising perceived inequity is to change the basis of the assessment. Thus, for example, someone may perceive that they are poorly paid in comparison with others performing work assessed as similar, but on reflection may rationalise this and restore balance and equity by reflecting on other benefits that their job provides that may not be present in their comparitors. For example, their job may be perceived as providing much greater security than others or providing better opportunities for training and advancement or be performed in a more congenial environment than that enjoyed by many others with whom they have compared themselves. Thus equity and motivation are restored by changing the basis of comparison.

- *Leave the job.* Continued feelings of inequity which cannot be restored by altering any of the above cause internal tension which can ultimately only be relieved by leaving the organisation and finding a new job that meets our perceptions of fair outcomes in relation to inputs. Thus Adams provides a theoretical perspective on labour turnover by explaining it in terms of perceived inequity, though the causes of inequity will vary from person to person and may include both intrinsic and extrinsic rewards.

Like expectancy theory, equity theory indicates that the causes of work motivation are complex and do not lie in the design of jobs alone. Varying from individual to individual, some people will be motivated by intrinsic job satisfaction and an inability to achieve this desired outcome could create inequity and result in their leaving the organisation. For others, however, other extrinsic factors (such as pay, status, security, good working conditions, etc.) may be more important outcomes and any failure to achieve these could have a similar effect. Both expectancy theory and equity theory provide useful reminders that job design and job satisfaction do not provide the full answer to issues of motivation and retention and that attention to a wide range of factors in human resource policies and practices is needed to meet the motivational needs of all staff. These may include good working conditions, opportunities for social interaction, opportunities for personal growth and development, participative management styles, fair pay and grading systems, competitive salaries and benefits, and so on.

Another highly influential idea from the process theorists is known as the *goal theory* motivation and is associated with Locke and Latham (1984, 1990). The theory is based on the notion that the achievement of goals is an important driver of human behaviour and therefore a major factor in explaining motivation. The theory also has the advantage of being readily applicable in the workplace and contains what many managers would see as sound common sense.

Goal theory recognises that setting goals to achieve is an integral part of day-to-day management. Goals may be set in a variety of ways. They may be set quite informally by a supervisor who tells an employee what a task is and what needs to be done. They may be set more formally by a training instructor or at a training course. They may be set between employee and manager at meetings which establish forthcoming workloads. They may be set and reviewed at formal performance appraisal meetings and they may also form part of a system of management by objectives. In whatever context goals are set, Locke's research has established certain principles that need to be built into the goal-setting process and, if built in, will have the effect of motivating employees to achieve the goals agreed. Conversely, if these principles are not built in, goal-setting will not have a motivating effect.

The motivating principles which Locke advocates should be incorporated into all goal setting processes are as follows:

1. *Goals should be stretching.* The setting of difficult goals leads to higher performance than easy goals.

2. *Goals should be measurable.* Specific or measurable goals lead to higher performance than 'do your best goals': measures may include volumes, timescales, quality targets, cost constraints, customer satisfaction measures, etc., but it is vital that there is

some yardstick against which an individual can measure and assess their performance.

3. *Goal achievement needs feedback on progress.* Knowledge of progress or feedback on a regular basis during the process of goal achievement leads to higher performance than when no feedback is provided.

4. *Goal-setting requires employee involvement.* Employee involvement or participation in setting goals to be achieved will create greater commitment to them than when goals are imposed without joint agreement between employee and manager.

5. *Goal-setting requires self-generated feedback.* Opportunities for self-generated feedback (e.g. self-appraisal) are more powerful motivators for the achievement of goals than manager-generated feedback.

6. *Goal commitment increases when goals are made public.* The more goals to be achieved by an individual are shared with and known to others in a work team or beyond, the greater the commitment of an individual to the achievement of their goals.

7. *Goal achievement is enhanced by self-efficacy.* Self-efficacy refers to an individual's belief in their capability to succeed and to perform a task effectively and is likely to be enhanced by equipping employees with the competencies necessary for performing the role. Training and development is the main way in which this can be done and thus this plays an important role in Locke's theory of motivation through goal-setting.

8. *Incentives, rewards and goal achievement.* Monetary incentives may act to motivate where the amount on offer is significant and the goals set are seen as achievable, but where a goal is seen as unattainable, the availability of incentive pay will not stimulate goal achievement.

Goal theory has been popularised through the acronym 'SMART' which to some extent only encapsulates Locke's ideas about goal-setting. The SMART acronym states that goals should be:

- **S**tretching

- **M**easurable

- **A**chievable

- **R**ealistic

- **T**ime-bounded (i.e. with a set timeframe for completion).

An alternative acronym 'FRAME' has also been offered (Whetten et al., 1994, in Williams, 1998) and this states that goals should be:

- **F**ew

- **R**ealistic

- **A**greed

- **M**easured

- **E**xplicit.

In terms of job design, goal theory emphasises the importance of setting goals as a motivational device. Thus the characteristics proposed by Locke can usefully be built into our model of job design, albeit that goals are about processes rather than job content.

Socio-technical systems theory

While all of the above developments emanated from North America, in Britain a different line of research developed from the late 1940s. In the wake of Elton Mayo's discovery of the importance of groups as social units in a workplace, this line of research focused more specifically on designing and redesigning work around groups or teams. Originally associated with the work of the Tavistock Institute (e.g. Trist et al., 1963), the organisation of work is seen in terms of a 'socio-technical system' and was originally concerned with the impact of new, automated technologies in a workplace. The researchers from the Tavistock Institute observed that traditional Taylorist scientific management had offered technologically driven solutions to work organisation, the best known example being 'Fordism', named after Henry Ford who pioneered the production line for car manufacture, in effect putting Taylor's principles into practice in the context of a flow line. The early work of the Tavistock Institute was in the British coal industry. They observed that prior to the introduction of mechanised technology for coal-getting, work teams organised themselves informally and without close management supervision at the coal face, work team members were selected from among groups of friends, new members were taught in the course of time to perform all the tasks required to obtain coal at the coal face and work was performed flexibly by all the members of the team as the need arose. With the introduction of mechanisation, however, management reorganised and split up these teams, assigning individual work roles after the manner recommended by Taylor, with each person responsible for one activity. Management were surprised when subsequently productivity did not rise as they expected after mechanisation. The Tavistock Institute researchers concluded that the problem lay in the break-up of the multiskilled and relatively autonomous teams. Their overall message was that job design and work organisation need not be driven by technology and that technological change presented choices, not imperatives. Their solution was that work could be reorganised on a team basis, retaining the previous flexibility of skilling and autonomy, even after the introduction of technological change. Work consists of 'social systems' and 'technical systems', thus a 'socio-technical system', and the introduction of new technology should be carried out in such a way as to maximise team autonomy. In summarising the Tavistock principles of job design and work organisation, Buchanan (in Buchanan and Huczynski, 1997: 573) states as follows:

Individual jobs should provide:
- Optimum variety
- Meaningful tasks
- An optimum work cycle avoiding undue repetition
- Control over work standards and feedback of results
- Opportunities to engage in preparing or planning work and develop auxiliary additional skills related to broader task performance (e.g. machine maintenance skills)
- Opportunities to acquire and use valued skill, knowledge and effort

- Opportunities to make a meaningful and recognisable contribution to the final product.

The organisation of work groups should provide:
- Opportunities for interchangeability of work roles or job rotation where tasks are interdependent, or stressful or lack perceivable contribution to the end product
- Opportunities to produce a whole product or perform a group of tasks which contribute to an end product
- Autonomy to define work methods
- Responsibility for work standards and quality of the final output and feedback of results
- Effective channels of communication, both upwards and downwards
- Channels of promotion.

The psychological requirements of job content are summarised as follows:
- Variety and challenge
- Continuous learning
- Decision-making
- Social support and recognition
- Relationship between work and social life
- Desirable future.

This pioneering focus on organising work around flexibly skilled teams has in many respects proved the more enduring and influential idea to emerge from all the perspectives on job design. Its results include the highly publicised examples of abolishing production lines for car assembly at Volvo and has more recently provided the intellectual basis for the relatively widespread introduction of self-managing, high performance teams (both of which will be discussed further below).

A summary of the practical implications of motivation theories for job design

The various theories about the factors bringing about motivation at work provide a wide range of perspectives, not all of which are compatible. Though some generalisation is necessary, it is possible to summarise the main implications of motivation theory for practice as follows:

- Intrinsic motivation, expressed by Herzberg in terms of motivators (opportunities in a job for achievement, recognition, variety of tasks, responsibility, advancement and opportunities for personal development and growth) and Hackman and Oldham in terms of 'job characteristics' for motivation (skill variety, task identity, task significance, autonomy and feedback), provide a useful set of elements to be built into jobs that may help to motivate and retain staff.

- Locke's goal theory highlighted the importance of setting goals to be achieved at work through a specific set of proposals about how goals should be framed and goal achievement supported in order for motivation to occur.

- Expectancy and equity theory reminded us that intrinsic satisfaction through job content may not be a motivating factor for everyone and that for some extrinsic reward (pay, status, security, etc.) may be more important. Similarly, Herzberg's 'hygiene' factors reminded us that extrinsic factors in the job context can be causes of dissatisfaction. Thus, strategies for motivation and retention need to consider both intrinsic, job-related and extrinsic rewards.

- Socio-technical systems theory emphasised the importance of organising work on a team basis, with relative autonomy to organise work, perform whole and meaningful tasks, to have opportunities to learn and develop new skills and have opportunities to perform various work roles within a team context.

Taken together, the various perspectives provide a fairly extensive body of knowledge about what elements need to be built into work activity for satisfaction and motivation. Some practical ideas about how job redesign operates in practice will be considered below. Before, however, looking at innovative approaches to job design that build in the characteristics discussed, we need first to consider traditional and conventional approaches to job design and their potential impact on motivation and retention.

Traditional methods of job design

Traditional methods of job design, which originally evolved during the emergence of large-scale production in the late nineteenth century and expanded with the growth of production lines and mass production in the twentieth century, remain influential. It has also been argued that the same principles are widely applied beyond manufacturing or assembly lines to encompass office, technical and managerial work (Braverman, 1974). The basic principles of traditional job design were first set out by F.W. Taylor at the turn of the twentieth century in his scheme of 'scientific management' and they are based on the principles of specialisation and functionalisation. The principles advocated by Taylor for designing jobs may be summarised as follows (Buchanan and Huczynski, 1997):

1. Decide the optimum degree of task fragmentation, breaking complex operations into their simplest components.

2. Determine the 'one best way' to perform each activity through techniques of method and time study and design the workplace layout to eliminate unnecessary movements.

3. Train workers to follow exactly the methods devised and stimulate them to produce at high levels of output through bonus or incentive schemes.

The logic underpinning traditional job design is first that management alone should take full responsibility for all aspects of work organisation, with minimal decision-making within tightly defined boundaries being permitted below management or supervisory levels. The second principle is concerned with specialisation and achieving the appropriate 'division of labour'. Management itself should be organised according to functional specialism, referred to as functional organisation, and the performance of all other tasks should also be driven by the same principle of specialisation, the underlying logic being that people cannot be experts at everything and specialisation enables them to become competent within a restricted field of knowledge. The main advantages of this approach are as follows (Buchanan and Huczynski, 1997):

- Employees do not need time-consuming and costly training when tasks are fragmented and simplified, and can become proficient quickly.

- Leavers can quickly and readily be replaced because skills requirements and training are minimal, less skilled employees are readily available on the labour market and the production process is not disrupted by labour turnover or skills shortage problems.

- Specialisation increases the speed with which tasks can be carried out because people quickly become proficient in the limited range of activities required of them.

- Low skills requirements result in lower wage rates and lower labour costs.

- Decision-making rightly belongs with management, who have the relevant training and expertise, not with operatives, clerical or administrative staff who lack these attributes.

However, significant disadvantages have also become apparent with the traditional approach in a context of higher educational attainments and aspirations on the part of the workforce, including:

- repetitive and boring work generating minimal commitment to the job or the organisation;

- a lack of attention to quality of work, especially where output incentives based on volumes of work operate;

- a rigid and inflexible skills base, creating a workforce unfamiliar with learning more than what is required for routine work, ill-equipped for coping with an environment of rapid change and consequently often resistant to it because it threatens the narrow skills sets on which their livelihoods are based.

New perspectives on job design

On the basis of ideas emerging from the motivation theorists and the proposals for semi-autonomous teamworking presented above, a number of approaches and techniques have been offered to put these ideas into practice. Sometimes referred to as the 'Quality of Worklife Movement' (Buchanan, in Sisson, 1994), their ideas are based partly on idealism and partly on the belief that job redesign has an important part to play in raising job satisfaction and productivity and reducing absence and labour turnover. The QWL movement represented a reaction against the predominance of Taylor's scientific management approach to job design, the traditional approach, and advocated various alternatives. First, task variety could be enhanced through 'job rotation', one of the simplest approaches to job redesign involving rotating staff around a greater variety of activities. Second, they advocated that tasks could be broadened horizontally by adding a wider range of related activities at the same or similar level of responsibility, referred to as 'job enlargement'. Thirdly, some advocated broadening tasks vertically by devolving greater responsibility from above, referred to as 'job enrichment'. This latter technique was developed by Herzberg who saw it as the natural extension of his ideas on motivation in which elements contained in the job itself (variety, autonomy, responsibility, achievement, personal growth) rather than in the job environment (pay, working conditions, status, relations with colleagues, etc.) were of central importance. Finally, and perhaps most influentially, the ideas associated with semi-autonomous teamworking re-emerged in the 1980s and 1990s in what has been termed 'self-managing' or 'high-performance' work teams. Each of these approaches will be considered below.

Job rotation

Job rotation involves rotating employees between tasks of a similar level of complexity in order to provide some additional variety and reduce boredom. Job rotation may be introduced on a formal basis, with changes being rostered by management according to some pre-defined pattern or cycle, or be operated informally by a group of workers performing related activities with or without explicit management agreement. Its use may be particularly relevant where certain tasks are seen as less congenial and therefore less popular than others. The use of job rotation organised autonomously by a team of workers gives this approach some of the characteristics of autonomous teamworking in that it provides more opportunities for teams to decide who will carry out which tasks and provides some flexibility for team members to either participate in rotation or perform the same daily tasks (Buchanan, in Sisson, 1994; Robbins, 1993; Bailey, 1983).

Job rotation is generally seen as a rather limited form of job redesign, especially if imposed by management. In practice, it may mean that employees are rotated through a range of similarly uninteresting roles, doing little to enhance variety, motivation or job satisfaction. On the other hand, where different tasks provide real opportunities to do different things and acquire new skills, job rotation can increase flexibility and provide learning opportunities. It is worth bearing in mind that job rotation has been a long-used concept in management development, involving the rotation of managers through various organisational roles in order to broaden their experience (Harrison, 1992).

A number of issues need to be considered when considering the introduction of job rotation. The first concerns the potential disruption to employees' social relationships at work. For many, particularly where the work is relatively routine, the opportunities to interact socially with particular colleagues may be an important aspect of daily life at work and there have been examples of resistance to the imposition of job rotation where it would have meant disruption of these established relationships. Other issues to consider are possible increases in training costs, initial loss of productivity when employees are learning the new roles to which they have been rotated and the raising of expectations on the part of employees that their additional skills and flexibility may need to be recognised financially.

Some of the benefits identified where job rotation has been introduced have included significant falls in labour turnover, greater flexibility of cover when employees are absent, increased motivation and the opportunities to acquire new skills.

Job enlargement

Sometimes referred to as 'horizontal job redesign', job enlargement involves adding to the range of activities performed by an employee at broadly the same level of responsibility. Like job rotation, it is often directed at the problem of boredom faced by employees when carrying out a narrow and routine range of tasks on a day-to-day basis or short-cycle operations involving frequent repetition every few minutes. The implementation of job enlargement requires a job to be viewed in the context of related tasks being performed around it and taking a more holistic view of how the work could be performed. Thus, for example, if three customer advice lines were operated by three separate operatives, each dealing with advice on a separate product, a job enlargement perspective would question whether this was necessary. The solution might be to train all three operatives on all products so that all three were capable of answering any question put by any customer. Such an approach could have the effect of increasing job variety and interest, increasing knowledge and improving flexibility of cover when any member of the team was absent. As with job rotation, additional training and learning costs would be incurred, but these may be outweighed by other potential benefits. Some of the reported benefits of job enlargement have included reduced staffing levels and higher productivity, improved quality, better cover as a result of greater flexibility and lower labour turnover (Bailey, 1983; Robbins, 1993).

One criticism of job enlargement is that it does not go far enough in expanding the boundaries of existing roles. If the horizontal boundaries of jobs are being questioned, why not also their vertical boundaries (Bailey, 1983)? In the example of the advice line operators given above, this might also include a consideration of what their supervisor does and whether some of their responsibilities could not be devolved and built into the operators' roles. If, for example, the decision-making authority of the operators were limited in some way and certain decisions had to be referred upwards to the supervisor, it might be possible to devolve more of these decisions to the people at the front line and provide a more prompt and efficient service to the customer. Such a perspective, however, lies in the realms of job enrichment. Going further, it might also be possible to envisage the three operators being reorganised into a flexible, multiskilled team, with considerable autonomy to make decisions in relation to customers and with the supervisor less concerned with close supervision and only required to provide back-up in particularly difficult situations. This perspective, however, lies in the realm of self-managing teams. Both examples illustrate the limitations of the concept of job enlargement. The concept has nevertheless been used widely in recent years as part of downsizing exercises in which, following staff reductions, the existing work has been reallocated among those remaining.

Job enrichment

Job enrichment differs from job rotation and job enlargement in that it is concerned with vertical job redesign, in particular with the devolvement of powers from those above and giving more responsibility for decision-making to those below, and has in more recent times re-emerged under the banner of 'empowerment'. In the main, it is not concerned with rotating tasks to increase variety or broadening tasks at the same level of responsibility. The concept was pioneered by Herzberg in the later 1960s and is directly related to the incorporation of Herzberg's 'motivators' into job roles. It is also congruent with Hackman and Oldham's 'job characteristics' model of motivation noted above (Robbins, 1993).

As with job enlargement, job enrichment requires a holistic analysis of the tasks performed in a given role and an analysis of the decision-making constraints that are currently imposed. These constraints are likely to include the decisions that have to be referred upwards to an immediate superior, but also to any other dotted line or indirect reporting relationships. Having defined the boundaries of decision-making in a role, job enrichment proceeds to consider which of these might be devolved into the role under consideration for enrichment. According to Herzberg, the following are the principles of vertical job loading or job enrichment:

1. Remove where possible close controls on decision-making while retaining broad accountability for decisions at the higher level. This introduces responsibility and personal achievement as motivators.

2. Maximise the amount of individual accountability. This provides responsibility and recognition as motivators.

3. Provide people with a complete, natural unit of work, i.e. a logical and coherent set of tasks and area of decision-making. This facilitates motivation through responsibility, achievement and recognition.

4. Grant additional authority and maximum freedom to make decisions. This facilitates motivation through added responsibility and opportunities for achievement and recognition.

5. Provide feedback on performance directly to individuals, not through their supervisors. This motivates through internal recognition.

6. Introduce progressively more difficult tasks outside the individual's previous experience. This motivates through personal growth and learning.

7. Use opportunities to assign individuals to special tasks or projects which either deepen knowledge in a specialist area or broaden it beyond an individual's current range of experience.

Using the 'job characteristics model' of job redesign, Robbins (1993) suggests the following areas for attention in job enrichment:

1. *Combine tasks.* Tasks which have been fragmented along the lines proposed by F.W. Taylor should be brought together in order to create a coherent and related set of activities in order to generate motivation through task variety and task identity.

2. *Create natural work units.* Combining tasks should lead to the creation of a whole and meaningful set of tasks which generate motivation because they create task identity and task significance.

3. *Establish client relationships.* The content of jobs should build in direct client relationships, either internally or externally, following the dictum of total quality management that everyone

has a customer. This increases motivation through autonomy to manage the client relationship and feedback from the customer.

4. *Expand jobs vertically*. Devolve responsibilities and control that previously lay at a higher level downwards in order to close the gap between the 'doing' and 'controlling' aspects of a job and increase autonomy to make decisions.

5. *Open feedback channels*. Feedback is important because it lets an employee know how they are doing and is also an important element in Locke's 'goal theory' of motivation. Feedback needs to be given by managers on an ongoing basis, not just at a formal performance appraisal meeting, and, as noted above, may also be generated by internal and external customers. The recent growth of the technique of 360 degree feedback is another technique for opening up communication channels.

Autonomous work groups and self-managing, high-performance teams

As noted above, autonomous group working has had a long history going back some fifty years, but during the 1990s it re-emerged as a highly influential method of organising work under the banner of 'self-managing, high-performance' work systems based around the concept of teamworking. The terms 'self-managing teams' or 'high-performance teams' are now the preferred ones, but the ideas are essentially the same. Thus, while autonomous group working continued to be implemented mainly on a limited basis up to the 1980s, albeit in some well-publicised cases, the growth of the related concepts of self-managing and high-performance teams thereafter in the changed conditions of the 1980s onwards strongly suggests that this was an idea waiting for its time to come.

One of the best known examples of autonomous group working was the approach adopted by Volvo, the Swedish car maker, which some years ago abolished the manufacture of vehicles by means of production lines and replaced this with team-based cellular manufacturing. Under this approach, each major part of the sub-assembly was carried out by a multiskilled team of eight to ten people in 'cells' or specially designed work areas containing all the tools, machinery and stock of parts necessary for completing their part of the process. Each team was largely self-managing and responsible for such duties as work scheduling, quality control and recruitment traditionally handled by a supervisor (Robbins, 1993).

During the 1980s, the concept of 'self-managing, high-performance' teams began to emerge into the mainstream. A number of factors combined from the 1980s onwards, accelerating in the 1990s, to make flexible teamworking the preferred choice for many employers as a method of work organisation. It has been suggested that as many as two-thirds of all employers have introduced some form of teamworking for at least some staff in their organisations. The factors which have helped to make teamworking central to the strategies of more organisations, with the consequent abandonment of traditional Taylorite methods of work organisation, include the following (Buchanan, 1992):

- The need to meet higher customer expectations for quality which were not well met by traditional fragmented job roles.

- Pressures to raise productivity and reduce costs, often summed up in the phrase 'doing more with less'. These pressures led to extensive organisational delayering of the management hierarchy, with responsibility for decision-making being devolved to lower levels nearer the point of production or the customer interface. Thus self-managing teams became the logical corollary of delayering and empowerment.

- The widespread global diffusion of new technologies and the growing recognition that competitive edge came from people, their skills and their ability to be more flexible.

- Associated with the introduction of new technologies was the need for people to adapt to the pace of technological change. No longer could there be skills for life, but rather learning has come to be seen as a continuing process. Traditional Taylorite methods of job fragmentation did little to create cultures of continuous learning, while teamworking, together with multiskilling, provided a more suitable framework.

- Modern, computer-based manufacturing requires less traditional manual work, but rather calls for different skills, such as problem-solving and the ability to learn and apply new knowledge. Team-based working provides a more appropriate framework for a cooperative, problem-solving approach.

The notion of high-performance work systems has emerged out of the ideas associated with self-managing teams, but also takes into account a number of wider changes in the organisational environment. These include the achievement of dramatic and permanent reductions in costs and equally dramatic improvements in quality. Extensive delayering of organisations was central to achieving these objectives, with many organisations adopting the principle of no more than four layers in their management hierarchies, together with the devolution of much decision-making to the work groups responsible for the output of final goods and services. Much emphasis has been placed on equipping work groups with the new skills required for these changed roles and adopting payment systems which reward the acquisition of skills and knowledge, rather than rewarding output volumes. Some of the key features of high-performance work design include the following (Buchanan, 1992):

- progressive multi-skilling so that all team members are capable of performing all the tasks required;

- flexible work systems such that job titles become less important or redundant, with the facility to deploy and redeploy team members between tasks;

- delayered management structures;

- much closer attention than was traditionally the case to the recruitment and selection of workers;

- encouraging and rewarding the acquisition and deployment of the skills and knowledge acquired;

- providing minimal supervision and a high degree of self-management;

- placing more responsibility for quality in the hands of the team;

- adopting a more open and participative management style;

- increasing the use of problem-solving techniques (such as quality circles).

An example of the introduction of high-performance work teams has been provided by Buchanan (1992) at the Digital Equipment Corporation's minicomputer production centre at Ayr in Scotland. Under pressure to cut costs and make the plant competitive with other Digital plants, particularly those in the Far East, the strategy was to abandon traditional production line techniques of manufacture and reorganise around high-performance teams, each with around a dozen members and each responsible for the completion of a whole process in contrast to the previously fragmented approach of building on a flow line. The key features of these high performance teams at Digital were as follows:

- unsupervised autonomous groups;

- each group responsible for building the full process, from the collection of materials from stores, to making, inspection and testing and handover to despatch, with full fault-finding, diagnosis and machine maintenance responsibilities;

- multiskilled roles, with team members encouraged to share skills, knowledge and experience, as well as the input of extensive training;

- a system of skills-based payment designed with full shop-floor participation;

- team involvement in the selection of members and appraisal through peer review;

- team-based policing of timekeeping, based on flexitime, without the use of clocks.

The benefits achieved from the introduction of this system included increased productivity, reduced time to market for new products, reduced stocks and increased quality. In addition, team members demonstrated the ability to acquire a range of new skills that might not normally have been acquired by shop-floor employees but which contributed significantly to both personal growth and team effectiveness. These included:

- analytical skills;

- interpersonal, presentation and communication skills;

- group problem-solving skills;

- group decision-making skills;

- self-management skills;

- process design and planning skills.

'Quality of work life' vs 'high-performance' perspectives on job redesign

Buchanan (1994) points out that the high-performance approach differs markedly from the 'quality of work life approach' (QWL) which was based largely around job enrichment and focused only on the work done further down the organisational hierarchy, but rarely impacted on its upper echelons. He characterises QWL of the 1970s as being concerned largely with the following:

- a reduction in the costs of absence and labour turnover and an increase in productivity;

- a main focus on increasing job satisfaction;

- avoiding any impact on management beyond first line supervision;

- a 'quick fix' applied experimentally to problem groups;

- a technique imposed by personnel management practitioners rather than adopted wholeheartedly by line management.

By contrast, he sees high performance of the 1990s as being central to organisational strategies for competitive advantage for the following reasons:

- aims to improve organisational flexibility and product quality with the objective of achieving competitive advantage;

- based on the logic that the effective use of new technologies requires more autonomy and investment in skills development;

- involves changing cultures at all levels and challenging traditional hierarchies and methods of working;

- concerns longer-term changes to attitudes and behaviour rather than a 'quick fix';

- is fully integrated with organisational strategy and is not an appendage tacked on by personnel practitioners.

In conclusion, closer attention to job design as part of a retention strategy helps organisations tackle a range of issues which were identified in Chapter 4 as significant causes of turnover: employees' needs for interesting and challenging work (Bevan, 1991; IDS, 2000); opportunities for training in and development of new skills (Reed, 1998; IRS, 1999a; PricewaterhouseCoopers, 2000); and opportunities for teamworking and participation, with greater autonomy to make decisions (Reed, 1998; Hiltrop, 1999). As noted in Chapter 4, research suggests that issues associated with a lack of training and development opportunities are among the most influential on employees' decisions to leave.

CHAPTER 7

Performance management and staff retention

According to Armstrong and Baron (1998: 7), 'performance management is a strategic and integrated approach to delivering sustained success to organisations by improving the performance of the people who work in them'. It is strategic in the sense that it is driven by corporate plans and integrated in the sense that it brings together a number of tools of human resource management, notably performance appraisal, training and development and, if an organisation so wishes, reward management. The close links between performance management, particularly its developmental aspects, and employers' retention strategies was evident in the results of the surveys considered in Chapter 4. According to the surveys from Reed (1998) and IRS (1999), attention to training and career development was the number one priority in employers' retention strategies and its high importance also emerged from the surveys from IDS (2000), Hiltrop (1999) and Pricewaterhouse-Coopers (2000).

A model of performance management

A performance management system can usefully be illustrated by a model based on Sisson and Storey (1993) as shown in Figure 7.1.

Performance management is based on goal- or target-setting and the way in which it operates, as set out in Figure 7.1, is as follows. The system starts and finishes with the corporate or business plans of the organisation. Business plans are subdivided for delivery purposes and cascaded to operational units (divisions or departments) of the

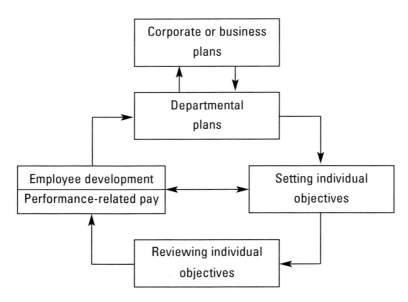

Figure 7.1 A model of performance management (based on Sisson and Storey, 1993).

organisation. The delivery of planned objectives is the responsibility of each departmental head who further cascades departmental objectives to each individual. This process is referred to in the diagram as 'setting individual objectives' and 'reviewing individual objectives'.

Since these are integral to the process of performance appraisal, the latter lies at the heart of a performance management system. Performance appraisal provides a vehicle for reviewing previously set objectives and setting further objectives for the coming period. It should be noted, however, that objectives can be set and reviewed in a variety of ways other than at formal appraisal meetings and the following should also be seen as part of the process of setting and reviewing targets:

- training or instruction in job methods;

- informal feedback on performance;

- performance standards set by quality control, safety or other operating procedures;

- performance counselling or related meetings called to review performance issues, set specific targets and monitor progress;

- the use of disciplinary procedures where an employee's performance continues to fall below the required standard.

Performance appraisal also provides a vehicle for identifying training and development needs and thus this aspect is integrated into the system. In Figure 7.1, training and development performs a role both in supporting the achievement of future objectives and in remedying any shortcomings when the achievement of past objectives has been reviewed. The system also provides an optional role for using reward, in particular performance-related pay, its function being to stimulate an employee to achieve the targets and subsequently also to reinforce and reward the successful achievement of the targets set. The loop of the performance management system closes with the cumulative efforts of all the individuals in the department feeding back into the departmental plan and upwards into the corporate or business plans.

Performance management is closely bound up with the notion of goal-setting. As noted in Chapter 6, goal-setting theory has identified that the setting and review of work-related goals can act to stimulate commitment and motivate employees to higher levels of performance. Thus the concept of a performance management system based on goal-setting is supported by empirical research into techniques of motivation.

It will be evident from the above account of a performance management system that appraisal performs a number of different functions and an issue arises as to whether all these functions can effectively be accommodated into a single interview. Randell et al. (1984) identify three important functions performed by appraisals:

- setting and reviewing current performance targets and identifying training needs;

- reward reviews which link appraisal to annual pay review decisions;

- potential reviews which are concerned with assessing future career development and promotional potential.

As noted in Chapter 4, all these objectives are closely bound up with issues which strongly influence employees' decisions about whether to stay or leave, including meeting training needs, receiving fair pay reviews in the light of effort expended and having opportunities to develop their careers. While many organisations wrap up all these objectives in one appraisal interview, Randell et al. (1984) and Fletcher (1997) point out that these three key objectives can conflict with each other. For example:

- Open and honest discussions about training needs, involving self-assessment, are likely to be overshadowed by the presence of reward decisions on the agenda and will tend to make people defensive when they feel that admissions about any short-comings may affect their pay increase.

- The use of appraisal to make annual pay review decisions often involves the use of rating scales in appraisals and these too add to the subjectivity of the process and may tend to inhibit open discussion about training and development needs.

- For various reasons which will be discussed below, an employee's line manager may not be best placed to discuss career development and promotion potential because of the manager's lack of knowledge of the organisation's promotion channels or the difficulties that an employee may experience discussing their aspirations.

The general conclusions are that each of these functions of appraisal should be separated into different discussions and take place at different times. Thus many organisations have separated discussions about current performance and training needs from reward reviews and some have adopted alternative approaches to career development. Each of these aspects of appraisal will be considered in more detail below.

Appraising current performance and identifying training needs

For Randell et al. (1984), reviewing current performance is the most important aspect of the appraisal process and the importance of this aspect is confirmed in Armstrong and Baron's (1998) survey of practice. Over 90% of respondents identified objective-setting as the most important aspect of appraisal and over 70% identified its importance in discussing employee development needs. A key issue in appraisal concerns what measures of performance will be incorporated and again the survey provides guidance on practice. While objective-setting remains central to performance appraisal practice, Armstrong and Baron (1998) identify that increasingly more organisations are incorporating competency assessment in their appraisal schemes, with around one-third doing so according to the results of the survey. Thus current practice in appraisal involves an assessment of both outcomes of (achievement of objectives) and inputs to a job (in terms of skills, knowledge and competencies).

Another increasingly common feature of appraisal practice includes its use for personal development plans, used by 68% of organisations according to Armstrong and Baron (1998), who also note that their emergence appears to be a relatively recent phenomenon. They argue that appraisals are increasingly being seen as 'learning events' which require the full participation of employees in reflecting in advance of discussions on their performance and development needs, airing these at the meeting itself and producing with their manager a personal development plan which takes account of what will be learned both to meet immediate job needs and also to meet longer-term development needs. Personal development plans themselves become subject to review and evaluation at future appraisals

Randell et al. (1984) suggest that appraisers may adopt three possible styles and strategies towards appraisals. One possible approach is referred to as 'tell–sell', a style in which the appraiser diagnoses all the performance issues and training needs of the appraisee and uses the appraisal as a vehicle for communicating these to the appraisee. What is clearly lacking in this approach is the appraisee's participation in the process, with the attendant risk that the appraiser has diagnosed the wrong problems and imposed the wrong solutions, with little commitment to their implementation on the part of the appraisee. A second possible approach is 'tell–listen' in which the appraiser has again diagnosed the problems and their solutions in advance of the appraisal meeting, but is prepared to hear the employee's point of view. The problem here is that the appraisee may feel unwilling or unable to challenge the manager's assessment.

Thus Randell et al. (1984) argue for a participative 'problem-solving' approach to appraisal under which the appraisee is first invited to set an agenda, diagnose problems for themselves and then offer reflections on their possible solution, unbiased by the appraiser's opinions. This does not mean that the appraiser must agree with the diagnoses and courses of action proposed and Randell et al. (1984) suggest that a 'listen–support' approach to problem-solving may also be adopted in which the appraiser deploys counselling skills, for example by using reasoning rather than outright criticism, to encourage the appraisee to reflect on the viability of the proposed solution.

The role of reward in performance management

The traditional use of appraisal for determining performance-related pay (PRP) decisions appears to be in decline, according to Armstrong and Baron's (1998) survey, with 43% of organisations incorporating this as a feature of their performance management systems, compared with 74% of organisations in an earlier survey in 1992. Armstrong and Baron conclude that while the emphasis in appraisal has shifted towards development and away from the financial reward aspects, nevertheless reward reviews within performance appraisal continue to feature prominently in the practices of organisations.

It was noted earlier that there are a number of potential disadvantages in interlinking current performance reviews and reward reviews and these have led many organisations to separate the two discussions. If, however, an organisation operates a system of performance-related pay which involves making assessments of performance directly linked to an annual pay review, there is logic in using the appraisal for this purpose since it is the main tool of performance assessment. The linkage of PRP to appraisal raises another issue which will influence the effectiveness of the interview, the use of rating scales. Because many PRP schemes are based on generating a rating which directly determines the amount of a pay increase, rating scales become a feature of the appraisal scheme. The use of rating scales, however, contains many problems of subjectivity and exposes the process to bias. For example, performance seen by one manager as 'excellent' may only be seen by another as 'above average' because of variations in the strictness or leniency of people's judgements. A further issue is that the annual appraisal comes to be seen by staff as about judging them, not developing them, and the issue of pay and the rating scales associated with determining PRP overshadow the whole process, with negative outcomes in terms of employees' open and honest participation in the process (Goss, 1994). Thus, organisations should question whether they really need to incorporate rating scales at all in appraisals, but where there is a case to do so in order to make PRP decisions, then some separation of the performance review and the reward review should be considered.

Beyond the issue of interlinking performance appraisal and pay reviews, there are number of other aspects of an organisation's reward management that might usefully be considered as part of a retention strategy. These are considered in outline below.

Market rate surveys

It was noted in Chapter 4 that salary enhancement was a less frequent cause of leaving than is often supposed (Bevan, 1991) and the results of various surveys of retention considered in the chapter also confirmed that employers did not rank pay among the most important causes of leaving. At the same time, it was also noted that pay could be more significant where it was perceived as being seriously out of line with the market (Hiltrop, 1999). In order to help ensure that pay rates are competitive with the market, it is important to identify where our organisation wishes to be in the market and collect external salary survey data to check market rates and market movements for benchmarking purposes. Where formal salary scales are in operation, the mid points of scales are usually taken as the basis of comparison with the market, with mid-points being adjusted in accordance with desired market posture.

Job evaluation

While the evidence from the research de-emphasises the importance of absolute pay rates as a cause of leaving, there is considerable evidence that relative pay rates and perceived unfairness with how base rates have been established and pay increases determined are more important influences on employees' decisions to leave (Bevan, 1991). We also noted in our discussion of motivation that feelings of inequity or unfairness about the rewards in a job in relation to the input of effort and skill, which might include pay, could lead to demotivation and a decision to leave (Adams, 1965). The technique of job evaluation is concerned with assessing the relative worth of jobs in internal pay structures and with establishing a fair basis for determining pay. Though widely but not universally used, the introduction of job evaluation based on fair and objective criteria for assessing the relative worth of jobs may have a part to play in a retention strategy, especially if there is any evidence from an investigation of reasons for leaving that perceived unfairness in determining pay rates is a factor.

Salary structures

People's pay may be expressed in terms of a 'spot rate' in which the wage or salary is represented by a fixed rate for the grade or is determined by individual negotiation between individuals and their employer. Alternatively, pay may be expressed in terms of a scale from a minimum to maximum rate, with rules governing the method of progressing up the scale. While salaries individually determined between employer and employee provide flexibility to agree and review rates in relation to the market generally and the market worth of the individual, they run the risk of introducing inconsistencies between staff performing the same work. Once employees become aware of these inconsistencies, perceived unfairness can be a contributory cause of their leaving. Thus, in addition to evaluating jobs in order to establish a fair grading system, it is also important from the perspective of retention that clear and unambiguous rules are established regarding the manner in which an individual's pay is determined and how pay progresses within pay scales through the use of some form of graded salary structure.

Traditional 'narrow-banded' salary scales, often typically providing for a spread of 50% from minimum to maximum salary in a scale, may, however, be found wanting in changed organisational circumstances and may prove unhelpful in enhancing retention for some organisations. In flatter delayered structures which are apparently becoming more widespread and serving to restrict the number of levels in an organisation's promotion hierarchy (Kettley, 1995), the concept of 'broad bands' has emerged as providing a more appropriate fit in delayered structures. Fewer layers in a hierarchy usually mean fewer grades and broadbanding involves implementing a pay structure with wider scales, often with a spread of 100 to 150% between minimum and maximum in each scale (Armstrong and Murlis, 1998). In the context of retention in delayered structures, broadbanding offers more opportunities for rewarding lateral career moves or taking on more responsibilities at broadly the same level and may assist in retaining and motivating people who have reached the tops of their scales (IPD, 1997).

Performance-related pay and retention

Performance-related pay is an umbrella term which incorporates the award of pay increases to individuals usually based on a rating given at appraisals, individual or team bonuses or organisation-wide bonuses based on the performance of a unit or the organisation as a whole. Probably the most widely used form is individual PRP based on an appraisal rating and it needs to be recognised that the process whereby a manager rates an individual's performance is often subjective. Where individual PRP decisions are perceived as subjective, this may infringe individual expectations about fairness and equity, factors which have already been identified as a possible cause of pay-related dissatisfaction influencing employees' decisions to leave. Thus any investigation of retention problems and possible strategies for tackling it may need to consider whether individual PRP is helping or hindering, particularly where any evidence has emerged that this is a contributory factor in people leaving.

Armstrong and Murlis (1998) suggest that where retention is a key objective of pay strategy, other medium- to long-term incentives need to be considered in order to stimulate people to stay. Useful medium-term incentives include gain-sharing schemes based on rewarding value added over an annual period, or profit-sharing or profit-related pay schemes linked to annual profits. These can have the effect of retaining staff over a longer period since the payment of such incentives require the employee to have been in post at the beginning of the financial period and to have remained in it by the end of the period. In the longer term, retention can be enhanced through the use of share option schemes which require employees to remain in post and hold their share options typically for three years before trading their share holdings for financial gain. Some organisations with severe recruitment and retention difficulties, such as in the IT industry, have also employed the use of 'golden handcuffs', a bonus payable for remaining with the organisation for a specified period and paid at the end of that period.

The role of appraisal in identifying potential and career development

Appraisal as a vehicle for discussing career development needs appears to have more limited application in practice, with just around a third of the respondents to Armstrong and Baron's (1998) survey saying that this was a feature of their appraisal schemes. This does, therefore, raise a question about whether the remaining two-thirds of organisations give due consideration to career development and, if so, how this is done.

It was argued in the Introduction that changes in the traditional psychological contract brought about by downsizing and delayering now mean that there are fewer opportunities for promotion through upward career ladders, the traditional reward for employee loyalty and a major factor in encouraging employees to stay. Though the demise of the traditional career should not be overstated, one survey found that 55% of employees felt that their psychological contract with their employer had been breached and the results were low job satisfaction, lower performance and an increased desire to leave their organisations (Newell, in Bach and Sisson, 2000). Thus the changed circumstances suggest that organisations need to consider more innovative ways of career development.

Some of the typical problems experienced by people in developing their careers have been summarised by Torrington and Hall (1998) as follows:

- a lack of information about career development opportunities in an organisation;

- a lack of feedback after unsuccessful attempts at achieving promotion;

- a lack of further development opportunities in the current role;

- waiting for 'dead men's shoes';

- a lack of opportunities for lateral or cross-functional moves.

In the light of these and other problems in career development, the case for initiatives in this area include the following (Torrington and Hall, 1998):

- makes the organisation more attractive to potential recruits;

- enhances the image of the organisation;

- is likely to encourage employee commitment and reduce staff turnover;

- is likely to encourage motivation and job performance as employees can see some possible movement and progress in their work; and perhaps most importantly

- exploits the full potential of the workforce.

Harrison (1992: 446) defines career development as 'an organised, planned effort comprised of structured activities or processes that result in a mutual career plotting effort between the employees and the organisation'. With a greater emphasis on 'employability' and 'flexibility' in the new psychological contract, career development needs to be a joint process with mutual benefits for both the employee and the organisation. Organisations need to be explicit about what opportunities are potentially available and how they can be realised, but with the emphasis on employability and flexibility, employees need to take ownership of their careers in order to equip themselves for opportunities that may arise either within or outside the organisation. Walton (1999: 217) explains the respective roles of employees, their managers and the organisation in career development as follows:

The employee must:

- Take responsibility for career development
- Obtain and use feedback on career options and their realistic potential
- Communicate career interests and discuss developmental needs with their manager.

The manager must:

- Support employees in their career development responsibilities
- Provide organisational career information and realistic feedback on employee career aspirations
- Encourage and support implementation of the employee's career development plans.

The organisation must:

- Communicate business mission, objectives and strategies so that realistic development can occur
- Provide employees with the resources necessary for development, to include on-the-job experiences, training and education
- Evaluate and recognise managers for their role/success in employee career development.

Torrington and Hall (1998) emphasise the importance of career management and planning being the responsibility of the individual, but summarise the following as actions which organisations can usefully take to help individuals:

- *career exploration* – providing tools and help for self-diagnosis;

- *career goal-setting* – providing a clear view of the career opportunities available in the organisation;

- *career strategies and action planning* – providing support to staff in planning and implementing actions for developing careers;

- *career feedback* – providing honest and open feedback about current performance and career potential.

Some of the measures designed to achieve better career development planning include the following (Fletcher, 1997; Torrington and Hall, 1998; Walton, 1999):

- *Career path analysis.* This may involve historical study and communication of information to staff about the job roles occupied by people who reached more senior positions in the organisation or may be located within a competency framework which includes feedback on current competency development and enables employees to see what further development is needed to achieve a role to which they may aspire in the future. Some organisations create career path grids or matrices which show how careers can be developed through upward, lateral or even downward moves.

- *Career review panels.* These consist of a panel of senior managers who periodically review appraisal documentation, taking account of both current performance and future potential, including the appraisee's wishes and the appraiser's assessment of their potential. Career review panels may also extend to holding interviews with candidates directly and discussing with them their aspirations and the possible career development opportunities.

- *Development centres.* These have close parallels with assessment centres for the selection of new recruits discussed in Chapter 3. Using work simulation exercises, and possibly also psychometric tests, candidates have the opportunity to demonstrate their capabilities and also receive feedback on performance, including both their strengths and areas for further development, which can then be built into a personal development plan. A variant on the use of the development centre is a career workshop which also consists of various exercises with feedback and advice at the end of the process.

- *Career counselling.* For reasons considered earlier in the chapter, an employee's line manager may not always be the person most suited to providing career development advice and, as an alternative, many organisations train specialist staff (e.g. a senior staff member from the HR function) to provide career counselling discussions.

While recent thinking about career development places emphasis on the role of the individual in maintaining their employability and has included lateral or even downward moves as potential options, Byham (2000) takes the view that current approaches are still too narrowly based on the concept of fixed jobs. In his view, 'it is impossible to plan future jobs with any accuracy' (ibid.: 40) and concludes that this renders impossible traditional approaches to succession planning which target one or two successors for each post. Instead, he argues for an 'acceleration post system' in which a group of high potential candidates are developed for undefined future posts. The implications of this for career development are that current roles need to be made more fluid with frequent changes in responsibilities and reporting arrangements, and people should be developed through stretching assignments with an emphasis on developing competencies and organisational knowledge and exposing people to challenges relevant to more senior, though undefined, roles. Rather than attending traditional, formal executive development programmes, learning needs to be more closely integrated into work activity, with more emphasis on feedback, coaching and action learning programmes.

In summary, some of the main options for developing careers include the following:

- lateral or cross-functional moves;

- secondments to other organisations or to other departments within the organisation;

- broadening the range and scope of duties currently performed or adding some responsibility for staff, for example to become involved in staff recruitment or training a new member;

- involvement in interdepartmental project teams, either on a part-time or a full-time basis, possibly also with team leadership responsibilities;

- undertaking of projects within the department;

- mentoring or coaching, involving working alongside or having opportunities to learn from an experienced member of staff.

The chapter opened by noting the importance attached by many organisations to training and career development as central elements in their retention strategies (Reed, 1998; IRS, 1999; Hiltrop, 1999; IDS, 2000; PricewaterhouseCoopers, 2000). Performance management, with its central focus on motivating staff through setting and reviewing objectives, identifying current training needs and developing an employee's career, can, if carried out effectively, help to address some of the significant causes of turnover identified in Chapter 4 and thus forms an important element in an organisation's retention strategy.

CHAPTER 8

Retaining staff through the work–life balance

The work–life balance is concerned with the increasing pressure felt by people at work to meet the sometimes conflicting demands of a job and other demands of managing a family, caring for elderly family members or simply finding time to balance work life with other interests or leisure pursuits. Though not exclusively affecting women at work, research in the United States has shown that managing conflicts between the demands of work and family is much more likely to be cited as a reason for leaving by women than men. The research indicated that around one-third of women cited such conflicts as contributing to their decision to leave a job, compared with just 1% of men (Taylor, 1998). A recent survey conducted in Britain by the Department for Education and Employment (2000) asked employers about the benefits of work–life balance practices and more than half stated that they lowered staff turnover and equally significant numbers said that they also reduced absence and increased productivity.

Given that women now account for just over half the UK workforce, compared with just over a third in the early 1970s, issues surrounding the work–life balance are likely to represent a significant cause of retention problems. Moreover, research has shown that the number of employees who combine work with the role of carer has apparently increased. Up to 15% of all people at work are carers, rising to nearly a quarter of people at work in the 45 to 64 age group, with responsibilities for looking after close relatives or children (Evans, 1998). Combined with the trend in recent years for women with young children to return to work and increasing longevity with more people likely to be performing a role in the care of older people, the need to find a suitable balance between work and non-work life as an integral part of retention strategy is becoming more acute. Indeed, these pressures have increasingly been recognised in legislation providing for statutory rights to parental and dependant leave.

The work–life balance also extends beyond issues related to women at work and encompasses the problems of 'presenteeism' and its corollary the 'long hours culture' which affects both men and women, with potentially damaging effects on individual health, family life and other non-work pursuits. Cooper (2000a) quotes a survey among British Telecom managers in 1998 which found that 38% would not accept promotion because of the perceived damage to their home lives and men were as likely as women to turn down a promotion opportunity. In consequence, BT has adopted the term 'lifestyle-friendly' policies to distinguish them from 'family-friendly' policies which implied, in their view, that the only people who needed flexibility were women with families.

In autumn 2000, the government put its weight behind a campaign to encourage more employers to adopt work–life balance policies and has supported this with a £1.5 million fund to provide employers with consultancy advice on the introduction of work–life balance schemes. It has also published a guide to good practice (Cooper, 2000a; DfEE, 2000).

The Department for Education and Employment (2000) defines work–life balance strategies as encompassing the following approaches to greater flexibility:

- family-friendly policies and practices which provide flexibility to combine work, family or other non-work commitments;

- working patterns which provide flexibility regarding working time or work location as alternatives to traditional, full-time or workplace-based posts.

Both these perspectives will be considered in the sections below.

Family-friendly policies and practices

The main thrust of statutory initiatives in this area has been to enable parents to take time off at the time of childbirth or adoption and, after, to provide mothers with rights to extended leave at the time of childbirth and also to provide reasonable time off as the need arises to care for dependants.

The present statutory position in relation to parental leave is that 13 weeks' parental leave is available for either or both parents at the time of childbirth or adoption. A minimum of one year's service is required for the entitlement and there is no statutory requirement to provide any payment during parental leave, though organisations are free to make some payment if they wish. The leave entitlement applies to each child and the entitlement may be taken at any time up to the date when the child reaches the age of five. Leave may be taken in minimum periods of one week up to a maximum of four weeks in any single spell. Prior to the implementation of this legislation in 1999, few employers operated schemes of parental leave on the scale now required, so the legislation has involved a significant change to previous practice. According to the CBI's *Employment Trends Survey* (2000b), 20% of employers operate parental or adoption leave schemes which provide benefits in excess of the statutory minima. Recent government proposals are for enhancing the current statutory provisions through the introduction of a paid element in the 13-week leave period of between two and four weeks.

As regards statutory maternity leave, the position following the 1999 amendments is that all women, irrespective of service are entitled to 18 weeks' leave. Statutory Maternity Pay is also payable, subject to the woman being employed at least six months by the fifteenth week before the expected week of childbirth, at the rate of six weeks at 90% of normal earnings, plus 12 weeks at a lower, statutorily prescribed rate. Where a woman has a minimum of one year's service by the eleventh week before the expected week of childbirth, she is entitled to 40 weeks of maternity leave. In all circumstances, the woman has the right to return to her former job or one that is substantially similar. Recent government proposals are to extend the minimum maternity leave period to six months with pay.

As regards the introduction of family-friendly policies in relation to maternity leave, a considerable proportion of employers have voluntary policies for enhancing the basic state provisions. Recent surveys have shown that around half of organisations enhanced the basic maternity leave periods and levels of maternity pay beyond the minimum levels provided for by law and also that this trend had accelerated during the 1990s (Evans, 1998). Typical enhancements introduced by organisations include the following:

- relaxation of statutory minimum service requirements for the basic entitlement or enhanced maternity leave entitlements beyond the statutory minimum;

- extending enhanced maternity leave and the right to return beyond 40 weeks;

- offering maternity leave payments beyond Statutory Maternity Pay levels.

The amendments introduced in 1999 also provide employees with the right to reasonable time off in the case of ill-health of dependant children, other close relatives or other persons who depend on the employee's support, disruptions to any arrangements relating to the care of children or close relatives or to deal with incidents arising out of children's education. No precise entitlement in terms of time off has been specified, other than that it should be 'reasonable', no service entitlement is required and no requirement to make any payment for the leave has been laid down. Surveys prior to the enactment of this legislation identified that leave for domestic reasons had grown significantly as part of employers' voluntary initiatives during the 1990s (Evans, 1998). In the light of the introduction of the legislation, nearly half of employers have introduced time off arrangements in excess of minimum requirements as part of their family-friendly policies and practices according to the CBI's *Employment Trends Survey* (2000b). Many employers will have introduced some payment for at least a certain amount of time off. Others will have introduced facilities for extended periods of dependant leave of some months' duration, akin to maternity leave or career break entitlements (see below).

For many years, a number of employers have recognised that many people wish to take extended periods of leave, particularly when their children are young, and return to their careers at a later date. Such extended periods of time off are referred to as career breaks which in effect are breaks beyond the statutory 40 weeks provided for in the legislation. The approach was pioneered by the major clearing banks in the early 1980s to encourage women, who made up around half the banks' staff, to return to their careers after child rearing, recognising that many women in whom there had been a considerable investment in terms of their training and development were not returning (Evans and Massey, 1986). More recently, in order to avoid this facility being discriminatory, career breaks are now available irrespective of gender and have been widened to permit both men and women to take extended breaks for other reasons, in particular to care for dependants, but also in a few cases for travel, study or voluntary work (Evans, 1998).

The existence of career break schemes is not widespread, with 11% of organisations having them according to the CBI's *Employment Trends Survey* (2000b). A number of career break schemes have eligibility requirements, including a minimum length of service (typically ranging from one to five years) and some require that employees have demonstrated satisfactory performance standards and also that they have the potential for promotion. Such schemes do not make provision for any payment to be made while on the career break and most specify a maximum period over which the break may be taken, typically from two to five years. During the period of the break, schemes incorporate provisions for employees to keep in touch. Most include provisions for keeping employees on mailing lists of in-house journals and other important briefing information. Some also require staff to come in to the workplace periodically for training and also to make themselves available for work for minimum periods, typically four weeks a year (Evans, 1998). Some schemes also provide a facility to transfer to part-time working or job-sharing (see below) instead of opting for the full career break.

The extent to which such policies assist staff retention is an important question and is one to which we shall return after considering the second aspect of the DfEE's framework of work–life balance policies and practices – flexible working arrangements.

Flexible working time and work location

The use of flexible working time and work location offer additional approaches to retaining people who might otherwise leave when the conflicting demands of work and non-work responsibilities have become difficult to manage. The use of flexible working hours requires organisations to question whether the only way in which a job can be performed is through a full-time occupant and to think innovatively about how somone's skills and experience might be utilised in some alternative way. Some of the options available are considered in this section.

Part-time working and jobsharing

Part-time working has for long been considered as applicable only in limited and highly specific circumstances. Such circumstances occur where the job itself does not require full-time hours, such as cleaning, or where part-time working is required as an add-on to the efforts of full-time workers, for example evening production shifts or providing lunchtime cover in retail stores (Evans and Attew, 1986). While such rather peripheral roles for part-time workers can still be found, the growth in interest in flexible employment has led to the emergence of a new role for part-time working: its use in preference to full-time working as a specific strategy or a greater willingness to consider part-time working where full-time hours were usually considered the norm. While cost benefits to employers may have been one influence on moving towards the employment of part-timers, clearly employers have also been responding to trends in the labour market in which more people, especially women with children, want to work part-time and the increased adoption of part-time working can be seen as the employer's response to changes in the labour supply and part of their strategies for recruiting and retaining staff.

While part-time working now accounts for a quarter of the labour force, the extent to which employers have adopted part-time working in response to individual requests by employees who want to change from full-time working cannot be gauged. It may, however, be observed that many more employers appear open to the possibility of employees changing from full-time to part-time work and more organisations are now employing increased numbers of managerial and professional staff on this basis (Croner.CCH, 2000). Around a fifth of female managers, for example, work part-time.

There is also the issue of whether refusing an employee the right to return to part-time working after maternity leave might be seen as indirect discrimination. Though there is no absolute right for an employee to insist on this at present (though recent government proposals may change this), any unjustifiable refusal by an employer to allow this has been seen in some employment tribunal cases as amounting to unlawful indirect discrimination on the grounds that such a condition adversely affects women. Particularly where a jobsharing arrangement (see below) has been proposed such that the job will be covered by, say, two part-timers, an employer must demonstrate sound business reasons why they cannot accept such an arrangement. The Equal Opportunities Commission have linked this directly to the issue of family-friendly policies and practices, arguing that 'employers have to show strong objective business reasons for not making jobsharing available to staff with family responsibilities' (Croner.CCH, 2000: 26203). It should also be noted in this context that the Part-Time Workers (Prevention of Less Favourable Treatment) Regulations 2000, effective from 1 July

2000, require all terms and conditions to be pro-rated to comparable full-time positions.

Jobsharing is a variant on traditional part-time working whereby two or more people jointly cover a full-time post and is an option offered by 36% of employers according to the CBI's *Employment Trends Survey* (2000b). The usual arrangement is for two people to cover the post working a defined pattern, normally a 'split day' with one covering mornings and the other afternoons, or a 'split week' with one covering say Monday to Wednesday lunchtime and the other the remainder of the week, or alternative weeks, each covering a full week on an alternate basis (Evans and Attew, 1986). Though jobsharing affects only around one per cent of all jobs and the vast majority of job sharers are women, staff retention is the main reason given by employers for using it. A proposal to jobshare often arises after a return to work following maternity leave. For the employee it enables them to combine child-rearing and work and for the employer it enables them to retain valuable skills and knowledge which might otherwise have been lost (Stredwick and Ellis, 1998).

Other variants on part-time working include term-time working or a 'short year' under which employees contract to work the weeks of the school year but do not work during school holidays. If the school holidays also coincide with times of the year (e.g. Christmas, Easter and the summer) when business is slacker, the employer may find that the work can be covered by staff working full-time; alternatively, cover may be provided by the use of temporary staff. Such arrangements can help to retain staff who might otherwise leave and find alternative employment where such flexible patterns are available. Term-time working is currently only offered by 12% of employers, according to the CBI's *Employment Trends Survey* (2000b), but this figure is up by a half compared with the number offering it a year before. A further variant has recently been used by the Health Service for nurse recruitment and retention. The Health Service has suffered considerable losses of expensively trained nurses to other occupations, particularly after maternity leave and during child-rearing, because of the unsociability of the standard hours worked. In order to attract nurses back and aid their retention, some health authorities have invited nurses to state what hours they would be able to offer and fitted an employment contract around those hours (Dinsdale, 2000).

Beyond part-time working, another well-established approach to greater working time flexibility is flexitime. Surveys suggest that around 10% of all employees work under a flexitime scheme, with high concentrations in the public sector (Stredwick and Ellis, 1998). Introduced originally in the 1970s to help employees avoid rush-hour travel, flexitime involves giving some degree of flexibility for employees to select their hours of work. The usual arrangement is that certain hours of each day (typically 10 to 12 a.m. and 2 to 4 p.m.) are designated as 'core time' in which employees must be present and flexibility is given for employees to start early and finish early, or start late and finish late (e.g. work from 8 a.m. to 4 p.m. or 10 a.m. to 6 p.m.). Some schemes also enable employees to work extra hours and bank paid time off in lieu, in addition to their standard holiday allowance. Such schemes have obvious benefits as part of any approach to family-friendly policies and practices. The flexible start and finish times enable employees to fit work around domestic responsibilities (e.g. the morning school run) and also provide facilities to accrue additional time-off to attend to further domestic or other emergencies. Flexitime can help attract staff with the need for flexibility to cope with non-work pressures and can help retention where such arrangements meet employees' needs for flexibility, without which they might seek alternative employment providing such flexibility.

Flexible locations: homeworking and teleworking

A further option when considering more flexible working hours and patterns in order to boost retention is the use of homeworking and teleworking, options offered by nearly a quarter of employers according to the CBI's *Employment Trends Survey* (2000b). For some people, home-based working provides an ideal solution to the problem of combining work and family or child-rearing responsibilities. Home-based working has traditionally been a feature of many people's working lives since time immemorial, in particular for 'homeworkers' engaged in the manufacture of clothing from their homes. More recently, teleworking – working from home linked by modem to the employer's host computer – has grown in significance and is now said to involve around two million workers (Stredwick and Ellis, 1998). In addition to reductions in office overhead costs, important objectives of employers in introducing teleworking have related to recruitment and retention (Stanworth and Stanworth, 1991). It has helped employers retain staff after maternity leave or in situations where one partner has had to relocate and has also enabled employers to recruit skills which are scarce in a given local labour market, but more plentiful elsewhere. Related approaches to teleworking are 'hot desking' where employees divide their time between the home (or elsewhere) and the office and share an office desk on scheduled days in.

A further, less radical variant used by a growing number of employers is to take a more flexible approach to permitting working from home from time to time. Survey evidence suggests that around a quarter of employers have introduced policies which permit employees to work from home occasionally (Evans and Palmer, 1997). Having instituted policies authorising managers to grant home-based working in certain circumstances, working from home arrangements are agreed between an employee and their manager. The usual circumstances will relate to the issues which might otherwise have led to dependant leave, such as the ill-health of children or relatives, but may extend beyond this to include other domestic problems or crises. Flexible policies on home-based working provide a half-way house between working from home on a permanent basis and granting time off, with or without pay, for family emergencies. Whereas such emergencies would in all probability been taken as self-certificated sick leave, a more open approach authorises the absence in return for working at home. In the short term, such a policy serves to reduce the frequency of absence spells; in the long term, it can help to aid retention since it legitimises the employee's need to take time off because of domestic pressures. Employees whose regularity of attendance causes them personal concern or who found themselves the subject of disciplinary proceedings might otherwise resign and seek alternative employment as the solution to the conflict between work and domestic pressures (Evans and Palmer, 1997).

Effectiveness of work–life balance policies as a strategy for retention

Given that conflict between work and family responsibilities appears to be a significant cause of leaving among female workers and a growing issue for male workers too, the introduction of work–life balance policies offer considerable benefits as part of an organisation's retention strategies, particularly but not exclusively where women make up a significant part of the workforce. Return rates after maternity leave have grown significantly in recent years, with most organisations achieving return rates in excess of 80% (IDS, 2000). Though changes to statutory requirements have obviously helped to increase rates of return, there is also evidence that the widespread existence of enhanced schemes of maternity leave and maternity pay, together with career break schemes, have helped employers to retain the services of valued employees who might otherwise have left. Dex and Scheibl (1999), for example, have reported that the provision of nursery places at Midland Bank increased retention and return rates after maternity leave from 30% to 85% over a six-year period. At Abbey National, a package of measures, including career breaks and bonuses payable after return from maternity leave, as well as the provision of more part-time and jobsharing opportunities, have improved retention and return rates from 55% to 78% over a four-year period (ibid.: 29). At Glaxo, retention and return rates have been increased from 40% to 97% through the use of the following package (ibid.: 29; IDS, 2000):

- enhanced statutory maternity pay, paid in the form of a return-to-work bonus;

- phased returns to full-time working by permitting part-time hours to be worked for one year;

- encouragement of part-time working and jobsharing;

- financial assistance with regard to childcare and also practical advice about local childcare providers.

In conclusion, family-friendly policies and flexible working hours and arrangements which help employees find an appropriate work–life balance have been identified not only as critical to attracting and retaining staff, but also an issue of concern for increasing numbers of people. Cooper (2000a) reports the results of a survey by PricewaterhouseCoopers of all its 150,000 employees worldwide which showed that achieving a healthy work–life balance was one of their staff's top priorities. Morris and Hodgins (2000) report the results of a study across many countries which identified that finding an appropriate balance between work and family life was put as one of the top three most important issues for employers and they conclude, in relation to tackling staff retention, that 'organisations are beginning to realise that due to increased competition for talent they have to be more proactive in offering employees a more inviting and rewarding working environment' (ibid.: 22). The evidence suggests that work–life balance policies provide one means of achieving this and in so doing they have an important contribution to make to employers' retention strategies.

Bibliography

Adams, J.S. (1965) 'Injustice in social exchange', in L. Berkowitz (ed.), *Advances in Experimental Social Psychology*. New York: Academic Press.

Alderfer, C.P. (1972) *Existence, Relatedness and Growth*. London: Collier Macmillan.

Armstrong, M. and Baron, A. (1998) *Performance Management: The New Realities*. London: CIPD.

Armstrong, M. and Murlis, H. (1998), *Reward Management*, 4th edn. London: Kogan Page.

Bailey, J. (1983) *Job Design and Work Organisation*. London: Prentice Hall.

Baron, A. and Collard, R. (1999) 'HR and the bottom line: realising our assets', *People Management*, 14 October, pp. 38–45.

Bevan, S. (1991) *Staff Retention: A Manager's Guide*, Report No. 203. Brighton: Institute of Manpower Studies.

Boyatzis, R. (1982) *The Competent Manager*. Chichester: Wiley.

Braverman, H. (1974) *Labour and Monopoly Capital*. New York: Monthly Review Press.

Buchanan, D. (1992) 'High performance: new boundaries of acceptability in worker control', in G. Salaman (ed.), *Human Resource Strategies*. London: Sage.

Buchanan, D. (1994) 'Principles and practice in work design', in K. Sisson (ed.), *Personnel Management: A Comprehensive Guide to Theory and Practice*. Oxford: Blackwell.

Buchanan, D. and Huczynski, A. (1997) *Organisational Behaviour*. Hemel Hempstead: Prentice Hall.

Buckingham, G. (2000) 'Same indifference', *People Management*, vol. 6, no. 4, pp. 44–6.

Byham, W. (2000) 'Pools winners', *People Management*, 24 August, pp. 38–40.

Chartered Institute of Personnel and Development (2000) *Labour Turnover Survey Report*. London: CIPD.

Claydon, T. (1997) 'Human resource management and the labour market', in I. Beardwell and L. Holden (eds), *Human Resource Management: A Contemporary Perspective*. London: Pitman.

Confederation of British Industry (1998) *Missing Out: 1998 Absence and Labour Turnover Survey*. London: CBI.

Confederation of British Industry (2000a) *Focus on Absence: Absence and Labour Turnover Survey 2000*. London: CBI.

Confederation of British Industry (2000b) *Employment Trends Survey 2000*, quoted in *Personnel Today*, 13 June, p. 67.

Cook, M. (1993) *Personnel Selection and Productivity*. London: Wiley.

Cooper, C. (2000a) 'Work–life balance', *People Management*, 11 May, p. 35.

Cooper, C. (2000b) 'In for the count', *People Management*, 12 October, pp. 28–33.

Corbridge, M. and Pilbeam, S. (1998) *Employment Resourcing*. London: FT Pitman.

Cranfield (2000) 'Recruitment Confidence Index', quoted in *Personnel Today*, 31 October, p. 67.

Croner.CCH (2000) *British Personnel Management*. Bicester: Croner.CCH.

Department for Education and Employment (2000) *Work-Life Balance Survey 2000*, quoted in *Personnel Today*, 28 November, p. 12.

Dex, S. and Scheibl, F. (1999) 'Business performance and family-friendly policies', *Journal of General Management*, vol. 24, no. 4, pp. 22–38.

Dinsdale, P. (2000) 'Nursing bank will keep wards stocked with nurses', *Personnel Today*, 21 November, p. 4.

Evans, A. (1998) *Family-Friendly Policies, Special Leave and the Parental Leave Directive*. Bicester: CCH.

Evans, A. and Attew, T. (1986) 'Alternatives to full-time permanent staff', in C. Curson (ed.), *Flexible Patterns of Work*. London: IPM.

Evans, A. and Massey, P. (1986) 'Sabbaticals, extended leave and career breaks', in C. Curson (ed.), *Flexible Patterns of Work*. London: IPM.

Evans, A. and Palmer, S. (1997) *From Absence to Attendance*. London: CIPD.

Fair, H. (1992) *Personnel and Profit*. London: IPD.

Finn, W. (2000) 'Screen test', *People Management*, 22 June, pp. 38–43.

Flanagan, J.C. (1954) 'The critical incident technique', *Psychological Bulletin*, vol. 51, pp. 327–58.

Fletcher, C. (1997) *Appraisal: Routes to Improved Performance*, 2nd edn., London: IPD.

Focus (2000) *Skills Needs and Recruitment Practices in Central London*, quoted in *Personnel Today*, 18 July, p. 8.

Fowler, A. (2000) *Writing Job Descriptions*. London: CIPD.

Fraser, J. Munro (1954) *A Handbook of Employment Interviewing*. London: MacDonald & Evans.

Goss, D. (1994) *Principles of Human Resource Management*. London: Routledge.

Guest, D. and Baron, A. (2000) 'HR and the bottom line: piece by piece', *People Management*, 20 July, pp. 26–31.

Hackman, J.R., Oldham, G., Janson, R. and Purdy, R.K. (1975) 'A new strategy for job enrichment', *California Management Review*, vol. 17, no. 4, pp. 57–71.

Harrison, R. (1992) *Employee Development*. London: IPD.

Herriott, P. (1989) *Recruitment in the 90s*. London: IPM.

Herzberg, F. (1966) *Work and the Nature of Man*. London: Staples Press.

Herzberg, F. (1968) 'One more time, how do you motivate employees?', *Harvard Business Review*, vol. 46, no. 1, pp. 53–62.

Hiltrop, J.M. (1999) 'The quest for the best: human resource practices to attract and retain staff', *European Management Journal*, vol. 17, no. 4, pp. 422–30.

Incomes Data Services (2000) *Improving Staff Retention*, Study 692, July.

Industrial Relations Services (1994) 'Ensuring effective recruitment: developments in the use of application forms', *Employee Development Bulletin*, no. 53, May, pp. 2–5.

Industrial Relations Services (1999a) 'Staff retention', *IRS Management Review*, April.

Industrial Relations Services (1999b) 'Benchmarking labour turnover: annual guide 1999/2000', Employee Development Bulletin 118, in *Employment Trends*, no. 690, pp. 5–16.

IPD (1996) *The People Management Implications of Leaner Ways of Working*, Research Paper no. 15. London: IPD.

IPD (1997) *Guide to Broadbanding*. London: IPD.

IPD (1998) *Getting Fit, Staying Fit: Developing Lean and Responsive Organisations*. London: IPD.

IPD (1999) *Recruitment Survey*. London: IPD.

IPD (2000) *Recruitment Survey*. London: IPD.

Ivancevich, J.M. (1995) *Human Resource Management*. Chicago: Irwin.

Janz, T., Hellervik, L. and Gilmore, D.C. (1986) *Behaviour Description Interviewing: New, Accurate and Cost Effective*. Boston, MA: Allyn & Bacon.

Kelly, G.A. (1955) *The Psychology of Personal Constructs*. New York: Norton.

Kettley, P. (1995) *Is Flatter Better? Delayering the Management Hierarchy*. Brighton: Institute of Employment Studies.

Latham, G.P. (1989) 'The validity, reliability and practicality of the situational interview', in R.W. Eder and G.R. Ferris (eds), *The Employment Interview*. London: Sage.

Locke, E.A. and Latham, G.P. (1984) *Goal-Setting: A Motivational Technique that Works!* Englewood Cliffs, NJ: Prentice Hall.

Locke, E.A. and Latham, G.P. (1990) *A Theory of Goal-Setting and Task Performance*. Englewood Cliffs, NJ: Prentice Hall.

Mahony, C. (2000) 'Ward winners', *People Management*, 28 September, pp. 36–8.

Marchington, M. and Wilkinson, A. (2000) *Core Personnel and Development*. London: CIPD.

Maslow, A. (1943) 'A theory of human motivation', *Psychological Review*, vol. 30, no. 4, pp. 370–96.

Mayo, E. (1933) *The Human Problems of an Industrial Civilization*. New York: Macmillan.

Morris, I. and Hodgins, J. (2000) *Staff Retention: Should I Stay or Should I Go?* Bicester: CCH.

Newell, H. (2000) 'Managing careers', in S. Bach and K. Sisson (eds), *Personnel Management: A Comprehensive Guide to Theory and Practice*, 3rd edn. Oxford: Blackwell.

Overell, S. (1999) 'Revealed: HR practices that really count', *Personnel Today*, 26 October, p. 15.

Overell, S. (2000) 'Policies must benefit all staff, not just the parents', *Personnel Today*, 19 September, p. 14.

Pearn, M. and Kandola, R. (1993) *Job Analysis: A Manager's Guide*. London: IPM.

Pfeffer, J. (1998) *The Human Equation*. Boston, MA: Harvard Business School Press.

Porter, L.W. and Lawler, E.E. (1968) *Managerial Attitudes and Performance*. Homewood, IL: Irwin.

PricewaterhouseCoopers (2000) *HR Benchmarking Report 2000*, quoted in *Personnel Today*, 31 October, p. 67.

Purcell, J., Kinnie, N., Hutchinson, S. and Rayton, B. (2000) 'HR and the bottom line: inside the box', *People Management*, 26 October, pp. 30–8.

Randell, G., Packard, P. and Slater, J. (1984) *Staff Appraisal: A First Step to Effective Leadership*. London: IPM.

Ray, M. (1980) *Recruitment Advertising*. London: IPM.

Reed (1998) *Rising Staff Turnover: How is Business Responding?* London: Reed Employment.

Reed (2000a) *Job Seeker Strategies Amongst Recent Recruits*, quoted in *Personnel Today*, 14 November, p. 75.

Reed, J. (2000b) 'The scatter-gun approach', *People Management*, 26 October, p. 69.

Reid, M. and Barrington, H. (1994) *Training Interventions*. London: IPD.

Rice, A.K., Hill, J.M.M. and Trist, E.L. (1950) 'The representation of labour turnover as a social process', *Human Relations*, vol. 3, pp. 349–72.

Robbins, S.P. (1993) *Organisational Behaviour*, 6th edn. Englewood Cliffs, NJ: Prentice Hall.

Roberts, G. (1997) *Recruitment and Selection: A Competency Approach*. London: IPD.

Rodger, A. (1952) *The Seven Point Plan*. London: National Institute of Industrial Psychology.

Roethlisberger, F.J. and Dickson, W.J. (1939) *Management and the Worker*. Cambridge, MA: Harvard University Press.

Sisson, K. and Storey, J. (1993) *Managing Human Resources and Industrial Relations*. Buckingham: Open University Press.

Skeats, J. (1991) *Successful Induction*. London: Kogan Page.

Smith, M. and Robertson, I. (1993) *Advances in Selection and Assessment*. London: Wiley.

Sparrow, P. and Marchington, M. (1998) *Human Resource Management: The New Agenda*. London: FT Pitman.

Spencer, L. and Spencer, S. (1993) *Competence at Work*: New York: Wiley.

Stanworth, J. and Stanworth, C. (1991) *Telework: The Human Resource Implications*. London: IPM.

Stredwick, J. and Ellis, S. (1998) *Flexible Working Practices*. London: IPD.

Syrett, M. and Lammiman, A. (1997) *From Fitness to Leanness*. London: IPD.

Taylor, F.W. (1911) *Principles of Scientific Management*. New York: Harper.

Taylor, S. (1998) *Employee Resourcing*. London: IPD.

Toplis, J., Dulewicz, V. and Fletcher, C. (1997) *Psychological Testing: A Manager's Guide*. London: IPD.

Torrington, D. and Hall, L. (1991) *Personnel Management: A New Approach*. Hemel Hempstead: Prentice Hall.

Torrington, D. and Hall, L. (1998) *Human Resource Management*. Hemel Hempstead: Prentice Hall.

Trist, E.L. et al. (1963) *Organisational Choice*. London: Tavistock.

Ungerson, B. (1983) *How to Write a Job Description*. London: IPM.

Vroom, V. (1964) *Work and Motivation*. New York: Wiley.

Walton, J. (1999) *Strategic Human Resource Development*. London: FT Pitman.

Williams, R.S. (1998) *Performance Management*. London: International Thomson.

Woodruffe, C. (2000) *Assessment Centres*. London: CIPD.